MONEY
HARMONY

Money Harmony

Resolving Money Conflicts in Your Life and Relationships

Olivia Mellan

WALKER AND COMPANY
NEW YORK

First published in the United States of America
in 1994 by Walker Publishing Company, Inc.;
first paperback edition published in 1995.

Published simultaneously in Canada by
Thomas Allen & Son Canada, Limited, Markham, Ontario

Library of Congress Cataloging-in-Publication Data
Mellan, Olivia.
Money harmony : resolving money conflicts in your life
and relationships / Olivia Mellan.
p.   cm.
Includes bibliographical references and index.
ISBN 0-8027-1285-1
1. Finance, Personal—Psychological aspects.   2. Money—
Psychological aspects.   3. Married people—Finance, Personal.
4. Communication in marriage.   I. Title.
HG 179.M427   1994
332.024′0655—dc20   93-37876
CIP

ISBN 0-8027-7456-3 (paperback)

Book design by Claire Naylon Vaccaro

Printed in the United States of America

2   4   6   8   10   9   7   5   3   1

Contents

Acknowledgments   *vii*

Foreword   *xi*

Introduction   3

PART ONE

The Individual Component of Money Harmony

1. *Getting Started: Finding Your Baseline*   17

2. *Your Money History: Voices from the Past*   34

3. *Money Myths: Learning to Identify and
    Debunk Them*   50

4. *Your Money Types: Dealing with Your Money
    Personality*   73

5. *Money Dialogues: Tools for Growth and
    Transformation*   97

PART TWO
The Couples Component of Money Harmony

6. Male-Female Differences Around Money:
Understanding Two Different Cultures   113

7. Couples Polarization Patterns: Resolving Power
Struggles and Moving Toward the
Middle   137

8. Couples Communication Techniques: Developing
a Climate of Respect   161

9. Structured Moneytalk 1: Sharing Your
Money History   176

10. Structured Moneytalk 2: Tackling Your
Money Conflicts   191

11. Goal Setting: Achieving Mutuality and
Money Harmony   209

Appendix A: Moneylife Quiz   219
Appendix B: Sources of Help and Support   221
Bibliography   223
Index   230

Acknowledgments

It is impossible to thank everyone who contributed to the evolution of my work on the psychology of money since its inception in the early 1980s. In this section, I gratefully acknowledge the principal colleagues and friends who helped make this book possible.

In 1982, Michael Goldberg and I created the original "money harmony" seminars, and together we conducted therapy sessions for individuals, couples, and groups. Thanks to him, my first and only partner in this work, I realized that, for many of us, money was the last taboo in the therapy office, and in life in general. In 1986, Mikki Woodbridge and I tossed around the idea of my writing a workbook in which couples could learn to resolve money issues, so she was instrumental in getting that first writing project under way. I wrote and published the workbook for individuals and couples in 1989 and used it as a manual in seminars I conducted for therapists and for the general public. My workbook and the seminars and sessions I have been conducting since 1982 form the basis of *Money Harmony: Resolving Money Conflicts in Your Life and Relationships.*

My many good friends in the financial planning community have been a source of encouragement as I wended my way through the new and sparsely populated field of money psychology. Larry Paul has been a supportive colleague, helping me to feel less alone in my work and giving generously of his time and his counsel. John Cammack attended my first money harmony workshop and introduced me to the International Association of Financial Planners and the community of financial planners. Peg Downey has been a great friend and source of support, and through her I learned about the National Association of Personal Financial Advisors and about fee-only planners. Joanne Bickel was my "good mother" in the financial planning world, cheering me on whenever I felt discouraged. Sacha Millstone taught me about socially responsible investing and was the first financial planner to sponsor a workshop for her clients. Betty Calhoun coauthored an article with me, and Mark Waldman shared radio interviews and other work projects with me with all his energy and competence. Victoria Felton-Collins, psychologist turned financial planner and author, brought me to California to give an early workshop on money harmony. She is one of the people in our field who share my vision of how to achieve money harmony for couples, and I am grateful for our ongoing warm connection. Alexandra Armstrong, a respected financial planner and author of a practical guidebook for widows, was instrumental in my conducting some workshops on the psychology of money that were geared to women's issues, and worked with me on the section of my bibliography that deals with personal finances.

Thanks to Helen Pelikan, a family therapist, and Bob Pelikan, a financial adviser, who conducted workshops with me in the 1980s and helped provide the Moneylife Quiz in appendix A. Annette Lieberman, coauthor of an excellent book about money for women, Ned Hallowell, coauthor of *What Are You Worth?*, and Judy Barber, a psychotherapist and business consultant who has helped many men and women deal with issues of inherited wealth and other financial matters, have also contributed a lot to the field of money psychology. I appreciate journalists like Grace Weinstein, who writes sensitively and sensibly about children and money and about the interface of psychological and practical money matters. Arlene Modica Matthews, a gifted psychotherapist and writer, has given generously of her time and advice (in the areas of publishing and money psychology). My friend Vicki Robin has been an inspiration to me as she, together with her life partner, Joe Dominguez, helps others transform their relationship to money and live in accordance with their most deeply held personal values. My new friends Anne Slepian and Christopher Mogil of the Impact Project also inspire me as they attempt to integrate money education work with political and spiritual concerns and values.

I am grateful for the moral support of several longtime friends who are respected authors: Michael Phillips nurtured me since the start of this work. His emphasis on the value of friendship has deepened my appreciation of all the wonderful friends in my life. Jim Fadiman has been a source of warmth and humor through the years. I am especially indebted to Warren Farrell, whose gentleness and humor about the world of publishing helped reduce my "publishing angst." Thanks also to Andy Schmookler, who was generous with his time and good advice; and to Michael Gelb, the most brilliant workshop leader I know, who helped me orient myself in the business world. My personal connection with all these talented people has given me a great deal of satisfaction and joy.

As a psychotherapist who particularly enjoys working with couples, I have been inspired and affirmed by the following people: Don Montagna ("Why Love Fails"); Lillian Rubin (*Intimate Strangers: Men and Women Together*); Deborah Tannen (*You Just Don't Understand: Women and Men in Conversation*); John Gray (*Men Are from Mars, Women Are from Venus*); Warren Farrell (*Why Men Are the Way They Are: The Male-Female Dynamic* and *The Myth of Male Power*); Harville Hendrix (*Getting the Love You Want: A Guide for Couples*). I have incorporated Gray's and Hendrix's exercises into my therapy work with couples over the years. Finally, my therapy work with couples has been heavily influenced by Isaiah Zimmerman, a clinical psychologist in Washington, D.C. By adapting his structured communication format, I have been able to guide couples through constructive talks on difficult subjects for more than twenty years.

I want to thank all the individuals, couples, financial planners, and therapists who attended my workshops and seminars since the early 1980s. These participants were willing to discuss their private thoughts and feelings on the sensitive subject of money dynamics in personal relationships. Many of them also took the time to write "money dialogues." I admired their honesty and openness in meeting these challenges.

I would never have been able to complete my original money harmony workbook without the editorial help of my friend and psychotherapy colleague Anne Anderson. Her patience, good judgment, and consistent presence enabled me to formulate the Money Personality Quiz in this book, and to keep at writing till the task was done. Vicki Haire, my calm and thorough editor, was my ideal nonjudgmental guide through the editing process. Ramsey Walker, Sally Hertz, Marlene Tungseth, and George Gibson provided help and support on every level. Barbara Monteiro was my "guardian angel," not only in the publication of this volume but in the realization of other work-related dreams as well. For almost twenty years my colleagues at the Washington Therapy Guild have been a source of strength and comfort through the twists and turns of our individual therapy careers.

Finally, thanks to my family. My husband, Michael Shapiro, has been my personal "money mentor" for almost a decade. His constancy, encouragement, and good advice helped me interrupt a hectic work life and persevere till the task of writing this book was done. My son, Aniel, is a true source of delight. He tried hard not to interrupt me while I worked at the computer and is at least as thrilled as I am that this book is completed at last.

Foreword

I remember a man in one of my workshops telling us how his mom used to say, "When the money stops coming in the door, the love starts going out the window." For most of us, the message was rarely stated that clearly; it was stated so subtly yet so pervasively that I call it "the invisible curriculum of our adolescence." I got the message this way . . .

As a teenager, I loved baby-sitting. (I genuinely loved kids, but it was also the only way I could get paid for raiding a refrigerator!) But then I got to dating age. Alas, baby-sitting paid only fifty cents an hour. Mowing lawns, though, paid two dollars an hour. I hated mowing lawns. (I lived in New Jersey, where bugs, humidity, and the noonday sun made mowing a lawn less pleasant than raiding a refrigerator.) But as soon as I started dating, I started mowing lawns. I was unconsciously learning that money equals love and, like most every boy, I was willing to take a job I hated to get a girl I loved.

That money represents love is one of the money myths Olivia Mellan confronts in her important new book, *Money Harmony*. Had I and my friends read it back then, we might have gained tools to combat our own latent fears and irrationalities about money. We would surely have come to appreciate with greater empathy the different money burdens men and women carry in our culture, often without realizing how onerous and limiting these burdens are and how they are exacerbated by myths we all too readily come to accept.

The gap between male and female socialization influences all of us but to different degrees and in different ways. And there are other messages about money we get from our families, religious traditions, peer groups, and our society at large that also control us. Understanding our money personality can help us understand ourselves and challenge our childhood messages and therefore the messages we pass on to our own children. Children get these messages more by what parents do, of course, than by what they say. If, in most families, Dad doesn't have the option of working part-time and staying home to take care of the children, while Mom does have that option, we internalize that reality as the way things should be.

Money Harmony can help change these unconscious assumptions and limiting beliefs. When we analyze our own money personalities in terms of these assumptions, we reduce our propensity to blame and increase our ability to understand our partner. By understanding our own personal money history, we also stop blaming ourselves for our own distortions and limitations in this emotionally charged area. When our own motives and influences are clarified, we can see ourselves and our partners clearly, perhaps for the first time.

Without money harmony, there is no peace of mind for the individual. And without money harmony for the couple, there is little marital harmony. In *Money Harmony*, Olivia Mellan gives us in one clear volume the work of someone who has confronted her own irrationalities and coached thousands of others to lift the money veil that prevents us from discovering our partner and others with whom we have relationships—and may have prevented us from loving ourselves as well. If the fear of looking in depth at your relationship with money makes you hesitate to read this book, then do it for the people you love.

—Warren Farrell, Ph.D., author of *The Myth of Male Power* and *Why Men Are the Way They Are*

Introduction

Almost everyone is uncomfortable talking about money. In my psychotherapy practice during the early 1980s, I became certain that money was the last taboo in the therapist's office—and in life in general. I noticed that my clients had trouble dealing with money objectively and productively and that it was harder for them to talk about money without getting irrational and upset than to talk about sex or childhood trauma. Couples in particular tended to polarize into oppositional attitudes and behaviors about money and attacked each other for their differences. If one thought money was the key to happiness, the other considered it a source of corruption and misery. If one tended to save, the other tended to spend. If one worried about money constantly, the other avoided dealing with money at all. If one wanted to put their money in joint accounts, the other wanted to keep at least some money separate. If one loved financial risk taking, the other was terrified of it. And so I began to help individuals and couples understand the sources of their differences and find ways to resolve them, so that they could make rational decisions about money and share goals for the future.

Why *are* most of us in this culture so knotted up about money? Because money usually represents so much more than dollars and cents. It is tied up with our deepest emotional needs: for love, power, security, independence, control, self-worth. And since so many of us are unaware of the emotional load that money carries, we fight about it, without understanding what the battles are about or how to settle them.

In the families we grew up in, few of us were ever provided with good examples of how to talk about money. Nor were we taught how to make wise use of our money. Our society bombards us with advertisements, fosters myths about the importance of acquiring things and "keeping up with the Joneses," and promotes instant gratification rather than teaching us about the value of saving, budgeting, and prioritizing for long-term goals. These messages contribute to our national crisis of overspending and massive debt. Many individuals exhibit the same chronic imbalances and tendencies to overspend. Others react against these models and become hoarders and worriers. When a spender and a hoarder come together as a couple, they form an uneasy truce. Conflict is a natural consequence.

What Is Your "Relationship" to Money?

For more than a decade, in workshops and seminars across the country, I have helped individuals and couples explore what I call their "relationship" to money. I advise them to think of money as if it were a person and to characterize their relationship with it. Is the relationship running smoothly? Or is it emotionally charged—marked by highs and lows, possessive feelings, worry, and anxiety? Maybe the relationship is a distant one, with the objective being to get out of it completely?

How would you describe your individual relationship to money? Your relationship to money within the context of your partnership with your mate?

Your relationship to money may be in balance or out of balance, but the odds are much greater that it is out of balance. Most of us must work hard to move the scale toward equilibrium, toward the goal I refer to as "money harmony."

Money harmony must come from within. It cannot be "bought" simply by acquiring more money. I firmly believe that if your relationship to money is out of balance and you come into some money, this relationship will be a little more out of balance. If you are an overspender, you will overspend more wildly. If you are a compulsive saver, you will save more compulsively. An avoider will just avoid dealing with money to a greater extent and end up with even more anxiety; and a chronic worrier will worry more intensely about it. So only by achieving money harmony can you put that newfound money to good use—or cope effectively during periods when you happen to have less money.

In the 1990s, you may indeed find that you have less money, or that the money you do have is insufficient to meet all your expenses. The current financial climate, which is fraught with the uncertainties and pressures that accompany a recession, has made stress and anxiety the order of the day—even when you have the money and the desire to make investments for the future.

Many couples today fear they will lose their jobs or that their salaries won't keep pace with increases in the cost of living. Others are juggling the financial burdens of caring for aging parents while sending their children to college. As women have entered the workforce in increasing numbers, a couple's "moneylife" has become more complicated than ever before, and women have assumed greater responsibilities in financial decision making. But with the proliferation of investment options, it's not easy for any of us to decide what to do with our money. We wonder: Are CDs now passé? Is today's "hot" mutual fund really the correct financial choice? And there's still the age-old question of how to maximize growth while minimizing risk. An additional—and very significant— complication arises when the members of a couple have conflicting money styles and different ideas about what to do with their money. It's no wonder that so many couples are confused and upset! Unless they take steps in the direction of money harmony, their chronic money styles will only become more severe.

How This Book Will Help You Achieve Money Harmony

This book explores the psychological aspects of your relationship to money. It will give you the tools to handle your money with more objectivity and confidence, whether you're operating alone or with a partner.

Let's say that you are a man who has been the chief breadwinner of the family and you are unexpectedly laid off after years of competent, well-respected work. You are feeling angry, scared, depressed; the number of fights you're having with your wife is at an all-time high; and you seem to be always yelling at your children. Although this book offers no advice on how to go about finding another job, it does give you the means to separate your current misfortune from your own sense of self-worth. It can help you remain positive and forward-looking, instead of lapsing into hopelessness as you look for new work. It can teach you how to grapple with your financial crisis so you don't need to take things out on your wife and family.

If you are a woman who chronically avoids balancing the checkbook, paying bills on time, and who feels overwhelmed by the tasks of money management in general, this book can help you understand and turn around these patterns of avoidance. If you are a woman who has just begun to make more money than your husband, and this is causing stress both internally and in the marriage, *Money Harmony* can enable you to come to terms with and devise strategies for adjusting to this new aspect of your money relationship with your spouse.

Perhaps you are in your second marriage and find that the scars from your previous relationship are having a negative effect on how you deal with money with your present spouse. This book can help you forge a new, healthier way of handling money that is not controlled by past traumas.

For most of us, our relationship with money is loaded and unclear. It is clouded with guilt, shame, anxiety, secrecy, and fear. By reading the chapters of this book, doing the self-awareness exercises, and practicing some of the assignments, you will come to understand and improve your own individual attitudes and behaviors in relation to money. If you are in a couple relationship, this book will help you learn to communicate honestly and openly with your partner and give you tools and insights to help resolve conflicts between you when it comes to money.

Part I is a detailed guide for exploring your individual relationship to money. In chapter 1, you begin by assessing the basic strengths and weaknesses of this relationship, and then take the Money Personality Quiz to identify your money type or types (spender, hoarder, avoider, etc.). In chapter 2, you look back on your own history with money, focusing on the people and events that helped shape your current attitudes and behaviors. Chapter 3 describes—and debunks—the common money myths (money equals love, money equals power, etc.); believing in such myths may be preventing you from handling your money rationally. Chapter 4 helps you explore the full range of your money personality and presents assignments in "practicing the nonhabitual" that will enable you to move away from limiting habits and attitudes. In chapter 5, you learn to create your own "money dialogue"; it provides a wealth of information on where you are today and where you need to go to reach a balance in your relationship with money.

Part II focuses on the dynamics exhibited by couples in their moneylife together. In chapter 6, you discover which male-female differences can cause conflict in couple relationships and come to understand the positive aspects of these differences. In chapter 7, you explore a variety of polarization patterns that couples fall into (e.g., hoarder vs. spender, planner vs. dreamer, money worrier vs. money avoider) and learn what to do if you and your partner are embroiled in a perpetual tug-of-war. Chapter 8 gives you a variety of couples communication techniques for creating a safe, positive climate of respect in which to discuss and harmonize your differences. In chapter 9, I walk you through your own "structured moneytalk"; here you get to know your partner's money history and share your own in a way that promotes intimacy. In chapter 10, you learn how to conduct a structured moneytalk on a loaded issue that you and your partner have had trouble resolving up to now. And finally, in chapter 11, you get some helpful guidelines for setting individual and joint goals.

The examples in this book are drawn from clients I've encountered in my psychotherapy practice, my workshops, and my seminars. But in the interest of confidentiality, names and details have been changed so the original people are unrecognizable. These examples will help you see how other individuals and couples have struggled with and resolved similar thorny issues around money in their own lives.

I believe that there are no universal rules on how to deal with money wisely. But if you develop a balanced relationship with money, or make progress in that direction, your satisfaction in life will increase. Furthermore, if you and your partner understand the dynamics of your moneylife together, have the proper skills and attitudes for communicating positively and productively, you can indeed move as a couple toward money harmony.

Although the second part of *Money Harmony* is designed to help couples, it can also be useful to other dyads such as business partnerships and parent-child pairs. In fact, any two people who are involved in an intimate and/or ha-

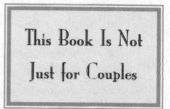

This Book Is Not Just for Couples

bitual relationship can profit from reading this book. Not only will they gain insight into the dynamics of their relationship, but they will learn valuable skills in conflict resolution.

Since there are so few "money therapists" around, psychotherapists will find this book useful as a guide to help their clients navigate through the deep waters of interpersonal conflict over money. In addition, many therapists have their own loaded issues as far as money is concerned, so they tend to deflect the focus away from money when individuals and couples raise the subject in counseling sessions. This book can help therapists feel more comfortable exploring issues relating to money, perhaps for the first time.

By reading this book, financial planners and other money professionals will understand why some of their clients freeze up or even bolt out of their office after a perfectly rational and sound financial plan has been presented to them; why couples sometimes have intense marital battles about money in their offices; and what steps can be taken to help couples resolve these struggles.

How to Use This Book

✹ *Read the chapters in order.* If you are in a couple relationship, don't skip the chapters addressed to you as an individual in order to get to the chapters on couples as quickly as possible. Unless you first tackle your own individual money issues, you will be unable to do your part in improving the dialogue and patterns of decision making in your couple relationship.

✹ *I strongly recommend doing all the suggested exercises.* You will get the most out of this book if you either write down or tape-record your responses to the various questions and assignments. You might even consider buying a notebook in which you jot down all your responses. Such a record makes it easy for you to track your progress as you move toward balance, both individually and as a couple. If you are not willing to write down or tape your responses, taking some time to think about the material presented in the exercises will still prove beneficial. You'll gain a greater awareness of your fears and irrationalities—and of your strengths as well.

✹ *Pace yourself appropriately.* Go through this book at a pace that will maximize your learning. If you learn best by processing information in small doses, reading a chapter at a sitting, or even a portion of a chapter, may make the most sense. If you do better by plunging in and devouring larger chunks of information at a time, you may prefer to read the book from cover to cover in a few sittings. Some of you may choose to make a ritual out of working with this book: doing the work at the same time and place every day, or every week. There are no hard-and-fast rules here; whatever pace works best for you, both individually and as a couple, is the right pace.

❋ *Less stress equals better learning.* If possible, read this book when you're feeling relaxed—and not when you're under the gun to complete your taxes or buy a house or another major purchase, or when you and your partner are right in the middle of a money conflict. The book will still be helpful when you are under stress, but at such times you can expect to revert to your oldest, most dysfunctional mode of reacting and will be less inclined to learn new behaviors and attitudes—about money or anything else.

❋ *Take a breather when necessary, but come back soon!* If you find yourself getting tense or anxious while reading these chapters, try breathing deeply and giving yourself credit for attempting to tackle these sensitive issues. If that doesn't help, take a break. But make a date with yourself (in Part I) or with your partner (in Part II) to come back to the book at another time. Don't drop your reading for too long or you'll lose valuable momentum.

❋ *Cultivate honesty and openness.* Be as honest with yourself and with your partner as possible. Of course, you need to respect your own limits, and those of your mate, when it comes to sharing the details of your own private journeys. You also have the right to stop talking about something that makes you uncomfortable. (Come back to it later when you are ready to try again.) Remember: The more you are able to share with your partner, the more intimacy that will result. And the more self-honesty you cultivate, the deeper your money harmony work will go.

❋ *Practice and monitor new actions and attitudes.* You will be doing a variety of assignments in which the objective is to sample new behaviors and attitudes in connection with money. I recommend that you take note of your reactions to "doing what doesn't come naturally"; write down or tape-record all your thoughts and feelings—both positive and negative.

* *Reward yourself for your changes.* When you do the exercises, or take actions that are new and different for you, either individually or as a couple, I suggest you reward yourself for this new behavior. Choose a reward that does not reinforce any of your old patterns (overspenders should not reward themselves by spending money!).

* *Give yourself positive feedback.* Take time to appreciate the courage and self-awareness it takes to grapple with the material presented here. I suggest you give yourself a pat on the back when you come to the end of each chapter—if not more often. It's impossible to give yourself too much praise; this feedback serves to build the reserves necessary for increasing your self-esteem and for making positive changes in your life.

* *Tackle issues with patience and gentleness, and in the right order.* Money harmony work is a slow and challenging process. Be patient with, and cultivate a nonjudgmental and forgiving attitude toward, yourself and your irrationalities. If you are in a couple relationship, extend this patience and compassion to your partner as well. Remember that you (and your mate) cannot realistically resolve all issues at once. I have found that if couples begin by expressing their thoughts and feelings about a sensitive money topic, they stand a much better chance of negotiating calmly and making concrete decisions that are acceptable to both parties. Deal with short-term issues that call for practical decisions before tackling long-term issues. The latter can be put off and approached more slowly.

* *Keep your sense of humor.* Though many of us have painful histories around money, it is important to keep the seriousness of money conflicts in perspective. I write spoof songs about money personality types to help myself remember that I share many irrational traits with

hordes of other people, and that dealing with money, even in a couple relationship, doesn't have to be an agonizing process. In fact, money harmony work can even be fun if you lighten up a bit and see the humor in your own foibles and those of your partner.

Ultimately, this book will help you see that money is *not* love, power, security, and so on. It is really just a tool that can enhance your life, both individually and as a couple. If you (and your partner) remember this, you will be able to enjoy the process as you move toward money harmony.

PART ONE

∿

The

Individual Component

of Money Harmony

1.

Getting Started:

Finding Your Baseline

Most of us have powerful feelings about money. These feelings can make it hard for us to arrive at rational decisions about our money and to keep our relationships harmonious when dealing with money. Some people feel guilty about having too much money; some feel ashamed of not having enough or not making enough. Others are afraid to deal with money at all, fearing that it will corrupt them in some way or make them feel inadequate. Still others worry constantly about money, and this worrying affects the quality of their lives, whether they have enough money or not. And some feel a kind of free-floating anxiety about money and have no idea where that is coming from. It's common for people to harbor a variety of feelings about money at the same time, and even to switch from one set of feelings to another (e.g., worrying and obsessing about money one day and then completely avoiding the issue of money the next day).

Just as our feelings about money can vary, so, too, can our behaviors. Some people hoard money; others spend it freely. Some are responsible about attending to daily financial tasks, while others avoid these tasks as much as possible. Certain individuals don't invest their money at all; others invest conservatively; still others take great financial risks. And finally, some people don't fit neatly into these categories and exhibit money behaviors that are contradictory (e.g., acting responsibly for several months and then undermining this behavior by going on an out-of-control spending spree).

Can you articulate your own personal feelings about money? Do you have a realistic sense of the money attitudes and behaviors you exhibit in your daily life? In this chapter you will be increasing your self-awareness as you gain an overview of your present relationship to money (its strengths as well as its weaknesses) and of your money personality in general. Doing the work in this chapter represents an important first step in the journey toward money harmony.

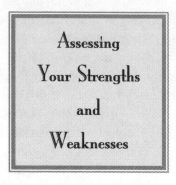

Assessing
Your Strengths
and
Weaknesses

Let's begin by coming up with two lists, one positive and the other negative. On the first list, note two or three areas of your moneylife that are a source of pride or pleasure. Here are some typical responses:

- I make enough money to live on.
- I balance my checkbook regularly.
- I'm a generous gift giver.
- I have over $15,000 in savings.

Now identify two or three aspects of your moneylife that cause you discomfort or even shame. Some typical responses might be:

- I go on shopping binges periodically.
- I procrastinate about paying bills.
- I bounce checks from time to time.
- I'm in debt.
- I have trouble spending money on gifts for me or loved ones.

As I mentioned in the Introduction, I recommend that you keep a record of your responses—either in writing or on tape. If you'd rather not write down or tape your responses, take the time to think about them.

After you have finished both lists, ask yourself which list was harder for you to produce. Was it the positive list or the negative one? Your answer will determine where you need to concentrate your attention. For example, if you tend to focus on all your negative traits connected with money, and feel bad about this, more growth and healing will come from acknowledging your positive qualities for a change. And if you tend to deny your negative traits about money (everyone has them, I believe, to some degree), you'll profit from focusing on your negative list.

Aaron, the self-flagellating hoarder. Many years ago, I gave a workshop in Washington, D.C. One of the participants learned firsthand about the therapeutic value of switching to a new perspective. Aaron was a freelance writer in his sixties who felt incredibly ashamed of being, as he described it, "a stingy, worrywart tightwad" whose wife and two daughters constantly criticized him for these qualities. His negative feelings were so intense that it was impossible for him to make any changes in his relationship to money. But in having to come up with his positive list, he was amazed to find that his hoarding tendency had enabled him to own a house and send both daughters to college on a paltry freelance writer's salary (his wife didn't work outside the home). Seeing his tendency to save money in a new light gave him enough self-esteem to focus on the aspects of his hoarding that were *not* serving him or his family well.

People never change when they feel too bad about themselves. Only by validating themselves for their strengths do they have a springboard from which to confront their weaknesses.

Mildred, the spender in denial. Mildred tended to praise herself for her generosity and to ignore the fact that she was overspending and running up huge credit card balances. Doing this exercise and focusing on her weaknesses made her uncomfortable initially but gave her an important insight. She realized how out of control her spending had become in the years when she was experiencing marital stress with her husband. She was, for the first time, free to make some changes in her angry, reactive spending habits.

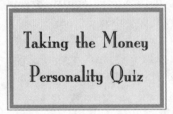

Taking the Money
Personality Quiz

Now that you have your baseline—a general assessment of your current relationship to money—and you know where you need to do your beginning work, you can move on to the Money Personality Quiz. By taking this quiz, you will learn which of five major money personality types best describes your tendencies. Bear in mind that each type has both good qualities and shortcomings, and that most people are in fact a combination of types. There's no need to worry about the outcome. Instead, try having fun with this quiz.

Record the answers on a separate sheet of paper. For each statement, choose the answer that strikes you first as being closest to your tendencies. There is no right answer. Just be as honest with yourself as you can.

Money Personality Quiz

1. If $20,000 came to me unexpectedly, my first impulse would be:

   A   To spend it on things I really want, including gifts for others.
   B.   To put it in my savings account.
   C.   To feel so overwhelmed that I'd put off making decisions about it for quite a while.
   D.   To invest it in order to make the biggest profits possible.
   E.   To give most of it away and use it to make the world a better place.

2. When it comes to dealing with my money:

   A.   I make sure that it never influences my life choices.
   B.   I enjoy spending it on gifts for myself and others, and on whatever will give me immediate pleasure.
   C.   I worry about it a lot and strategize how to make more and more of it.
   D.   I hold on to it and enjoy thinking about the security it provides.
   E.   I try not to think about it and hope it will take care of itself.

3. My goals about my money are:

   A.   To save enough of it now so that I never have to worry about my old age.
   B.   Unclear to me.
   C.   To have enough of it to ensure that I can buy whatever I want.
   D.   To have enough to satisfy my basic needs and then give the rest away.
   E.   To make as much of it as possible, as quickly as possible.

4. When it comes to following a budget:

   A. I rework my budget often to figure out ways to have more money to spend and save.
   B. I enjoy following mine closely.
   C. I take pride in living so simply that I've never needed a budget.
   D. I hate the word *budget*. I prefer *spending plan*!
   E. I don't have a budget and never want one. My money will take care of itself.

5. When it comes to spending money:

   A. I hope I'll have enough money to take care of unexpected expenses.
   B. I enjoy spending money, as long as I keep accumulating it at the same time.
   C. I'd rather save my money than spend it. Spending money makes me nervous.
   D. I don't follow where my money goes, and I don't want to. I focus on more important aspects of my life.
   E. I love spending money, and I tend to spend more than I earn.

6. I deal with financial record keeping as follows:

   A. I keep reworking my records, to figure out ways to make more money or to make my money work better for me.
   B. I'm not even sure which records I should be keeping.
   C. I enjoy keeping careful records.
   D. I keep some records but have trouble organizing them and finding them.
   E. I don't keep records. I hate to spend my time this way.

7. When it comes to saving money:

   A. I know I ought to be saving money, but I never seem to get around to it.
   B. I enjoy saving large amounts of money and spend a lot of time and energy thinking about how to save more.
   C. I have trouble saving money, and this bothers me sometimes.
   D. I save only for absolute necessities.
   E. Saving comes naturally to me. I am regular and consistent about it.

8. This is my attitude toward borrowing money:

   A. I try not to borrow money, but when I have, I find it hard to keep track of my progress in paying it back.
   B. I try never to borrow money from others.
   C. I'm willing to borrow large amounts if it will help me make more, but I worry about amassing debt if the profits don't show up quickly.
   D. I've borrowed money quite often, and I'm pretty casual about paying it back.
   E. I borrow only for absolute necessities.

9. When it comes to lending money:

   A. I'm pretty generous and don't worry too much about when I'll get it back.
   B. People tend not to ask me for money. That suits me fine.
   C. I wouldn't mind lending money, but people hardly ever ask me.
   D. I try never to lend money, but if I do, I expect to be paid back promptly.
   E. I don't mind lending money, if I get a good interest rate. I also worry about getting it back on time.

10.   As far as credit cards are concerned:

    A.   I prefer not to have credit cards at all. If I have one, I use it as little as possible.
    B.   I tend to use credit cards often and make the minimum payment.
    C.   I don't mind running up large charges, as long as I can pay them off quickly. I think about my credit card bills a lot.
    D.   I don't take much notice of the status of my credit cards. I often forget to pay even the monthly minimum until I get a warning notice.
    E.   I have always tended to avoid using credit. I prefer paying by cash or check.

11.   When it comes to providing for emergencies:

    A.   I don't have enough saved to provide for emergencies. I just hope for the best!
    B.   I have no money set aside for emergencies, and I almost never think about what I would do if something bad were to happen.
    C.   I keep thinking that I'll have enough to start saving for emergencies soon, but I'm still not quite there!
    D.   I've put aside a sizable amount for emergencies, but I still worry about them!
    E.   I try to save regularly for an emergency fund.

12.   When it comes to paying my taxes:

    A.   I scramble to get together some minimal records, just to get the taxes done. I'm always surprised at how much money I owe every year.
    B.   I save regularly for taxes, and most years I complete my tax return well in advance of April 15.

C. I hate focusing on taxes and try to get them done with as little fuss as possible.

D. I have trouble saving for taxes and doing my tax return, and I feel strapped every year before April 15.

E. I take pride in having more assets and paying lower taxes every year, if I can.

13. To feel totally satisfied with my income, this is what I'd need:

A. A few thousand more than I'm making now would be largely sufficient.

B. Increasing my earnings by a large amount every year is what satisfies me—$50,000 a year more would be nice!

C. I suppose I could always use more money, but I have no idea how much more.

D. I feel pretty satisfied with what I make right now. A big increase would make me feel uncomfortable.

E. At least $10,000 to $20,000 more than I'm making now.

14. When it comes to investing in the stock market:

A. I enjoy investing in the stock market, and I like to diversify to maximize my profits.

B. I don't think about investing very often, but if I did invest, I'd want someone else to make those decisions for me.

C. I choose "safe" and conservative investments.

D. I'm not an expert at investing, but I think it would be fun to invest in more speculative stocks that might offer a high rate of return.

E. I don't think about investing, but if I made any investments, I'd prefer those that were socially responsible.

15. When I want a certain item but it's not within my budget:

   A. Either I'll decide I don't really want it, or I'll buy it and figure out how to pay for it later.
   B. If I want it, I will buy it. I can always figure out a way to pay for it.
   C. I will buy it, whether I can afford it or not.
   D. Most of the things I want are not expensive luxury items, so I can afford them. If I do want something outrageous, I *may* buy it, but the purchase will make me feel very uncomfortable.
   E. If the item is important enough to me, I'll figure out how to adjust my budget to afford it. If it isn't that important, I'll forget about it.

16. When I'm feeling down in the dumps, spending money:

   A. Is the last thing I would do; putting some more money in savings might lift my spirits.
   B. Always cheers me up.
   C. Just makes me feel worse. Spending money has nothing to do with happiness.
   D. Is not what I think about to cheer myself up.
   E. In large amounts, and hatching plans to make more money, makes me feel better.

17. I would take (or have taken) a bank loan under these circumstances:

   A. To pay off debts, to go on vacations, or to buy something I really wanted.
   B. To finance my education—maybe. (I've never borrowed money, and I never want to.)

    C. To set up or expand a business, or to make an investment that would yield a high return.

    D. To make essential repairs or to increase my future security.

    E. To deal with medical emergencies or other unforeseen circumstances but not for anything else.

18. I worry about money:

    A. Never. I worry about *important* things!

    B. A little bit all the time. But I do all I can to manage it well.

    C. Constantly. It's the main thing I worry about!

    D. Only when financial crises strike.

    E. Not very much. I just enjoy spending it!

19. When I think about providing for my future security:

    A. I am quite concerned that I won't have enough money in my future, since it's been so hard for me to save.

    B. I have such a difficult time thinking about money that all I can do is hope that the future will take care of itself!

    C. Since I make sure I have a lot of money at my disposal, the future will probably be fine.

    D. Considering how systematic I've been about saving for the future, I feel reasonably confident about it.

    E. I don't think about the future in financial terms. I have more important concerns, such as my quality of life in the future.

20. If I won a million dollars in the lottery, my first reaction would be:

    A. To feel guilty, thinking about the starving masses who have nothing.

   B. To feel shocked, a little overwhelmed, and very relieved that my future was now secure.

   C. To be totally overwhelmed—I would have no idea how to handle it.

   D. To be very happy and pleased, and to immediately start thinking about how I could simultaneously make my money grow and use it for my own enjoyment.

   E. To be wildly excited, realizing that from now on I could buy anything I wanted!

Now that you have completed the quiz, here's the key to determine which combination of money personality types you tend to be:

H = hoarder S = spender M = money monk V = avoider
A = amasser

Refer to the following list as you score your answers, keeping count of how many H's, S's, M's, V's, and A's you've chosen.

1. A. S B. H C. V D. A E. M

2. A. M B. S C. A D. H E. V

3. A. H B. V C. S D. M E. A

4. A. A B. H C. M D. S E. V

5. A. V B. A C. H D. M E. S

6. A. A B. V C. H D. S E. M

7. A. *V*   B. *A*   C. *S*   D. *M*   E. *H*

8. A. *V*   B. *H*   C. *A*   D. *S*   E. *M*

9. A. *S*   B. *M*   C. *V*   D. *H*   E. *A*

10. A. *M*   B. *S*   C. *A*   D. *V*   E. *H*

11. A. *V*   B. *M*   C. *S*   D. *A*   E. *H*

12. A. *V*   B. *H*   C. *M*   D. *S*   E. *A*

13. A. *H*   B. *A*   C. *V*   D. *M*   E. *S*

14. A. *A*   B. *V*   C. *H*   D. *S*   E. *M*

15. A. *V*   B. *A*   C. *S*   D. *M*   E. *H*

16. A. *H*   B. *S*   C. *M*   D. *V*   E. *A*

17. A. *S*   B. *M*   C. *A*   D. *H*   E. *V*

18. A. *M*   B. *A*   C. *H*   D. *V*   E. *S*

19. A. *S*   B. *V*   C. *A*   D. *H*   E. *M*

20. A. *M*   B. *H*   C. *V*   D. *A*   E. *S*

Whichever letter (or letters) turns up most frequently in your answers is the one that represents your predominant money personality type (or types).

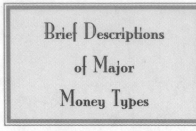

Brief Descriptions of Major Money Types

Hoarder. You enjoy holding on to your money. It may be difficult for you to spend money on luxury items or immediate pleasures for yourself and your loved ones.

Spender. You probably love to use your money to buy whatever will bring you pleasure. You may have a hard time saving, budgeting, and delaying gratification for long-term goals.

Money monk. You may try to avoid having too much money. You would feel guilty if a large amount of money came your way unexpectedly.

Avoider. You tend to avoid performing various tasks of everyday money management. You may feel anxious or incompetent about dealing with money.

Amasser. You're likely to be overly concerned with keeping large amounts of money at your disposal to spend, save, and invest. This preoccupation may be having a negative effect on your ability to enjoy your life in the moment.

Assessing Your Money Personality

In chapter 4, we will explore each money type in great detail. For now, you need only be concerned with answering the following questions:

- Which money type or types are you?
- Does your money personality cause you any difficulty in life, either as an individual or in dealing with your partner?
- What are one or two things about your relationship to money

that you think you might like to change or modify in some way? (When answering this question, note that the changes don't have to be actions or behaviors; they can be feelings or attitudes about money as well.)

Here are some common responses:

- I'd like to stop going on shopping binges.
- I'd like to start saving for my future.
- I'd like to stop worrying about money so much.
- I'd like to stop feeling guilty when I buy myself something.
- I'd like to stop feeling bad that I don't make more money.
- I'd like to stop feeling ashamed/guilty about making too much money.
- I'd like to figure out how I sabotage my own attempts to make more money, so I can provide better for myself and my family.
- I'd like to stop procrastinating about paying bills and doing my taxes.
- I'd like to be more conscious of where I spend my money.

After answering these simple questions about sources of shame, guilt, fear, and pride about money, and looking at the tendencies toward imbalance reflected in your money personality, you are ready to begin thinking about actions you can take or attitudes you can adopt to move toward more harmony in your moneylife.

I recommend that at least once a week, you choose one thing to do that will increase your self-esteem about how you deal with your money. The more concrete your action is, the better. I'll give you some examples of weekly assignments.

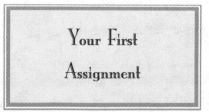

Your First Assignment

For hoarders:

* I will spend $25 or so on some frivolous gift for myself or my spouse.
* I will refrain from reworking my budget to see how I can save more money—in fact, I won't look at my budget once all week, and I'll see how that feels!

For spenders:

* I will put $20 into my savings account.
* I will refrain from going on shopping binges.

For money monks:

* I will buy myself something I've wanted for a while and notice how I feel about that act of "selfish pleasure."
* I will make a list of ways to use money that include giving to others and giving to myself.

For avoiders:

* I will keep track of where I spend my money.
* I will sit down for one two-hour session in which I pay all the bills that are due and balance my checkbook.

For amassers:

* I will spend less than fifteen minutes a day checking my investments.
* I will engage in activities that don't involve money at all, such as going to a museum or packing a lunch and eating it in the park.

If you choose to do one of these assignments, remember to reward yourself for this new behavior, and monitor your reactions to it. Give yourself credit for taking your first step on the road to money harmony.

Your next challenge will be to explore your history with money. When you can see how the past impinges on the present, you'll be in a much better position to make improvements for the future.

2.

Your Money History:

Voices from the Past

The purpose of this chapter is to help you explore a range of memories beginning with your childhood in order to gain insight into the influences that formed your money personality. You will be asked to answer a series of questions designed to jog your memories—about the members of your family; about your family's financial history, circumstances, and traditions; and about other influences such as religious training, peer pressure, and messages from society at large. By taking stock of *all* the past influences on your moneylife, you will become more and more detached from these powerful voices. This will enable you to relate to money as you alone would choose to do, in a way that reflects your fundamental values. If you are in a couple relationship, when you then join forces with your partner, you will not be dragging along a ton of excess baggage. Or at the very least, the baggage will not be hidden and thus can more easily be moved to one side when handling money or dealing with money together.

When I conduct my seminars on money harmony, early in each session I often say that most of us grew up in families where money was never talked about—in a rational, helpful way, that is. Before I add that last qualifying phrase, someone will inevitably object, countering: "Oh, in my family, we talked about money all the time!" But when pressed

Families Don't Talk Rationally About Money

to elaborate on *how* money was discussed, the speaker will tend to say something like: "Well, my father worried about not making enough money, and he yelled at my mother for spending too much." That's not exactly what I mean by "talking about money." I mean that it is rare to find a family in which the children are educated about the wise use of money, taught in a patient and nonjudgmental way about the value of saving, or perhaps more important, helped to understand some of the crazy or negative ways that our society and some people in it use money as a means of exercising power and control or as a measure of self-worth. It is perhaps equally rare to find families in which the children have any realistic sense of their family's financial situation. Many of us find ourselves adopting our parents' attitudes and behaviors around money without even realizing it; others react powerfully against these parental models, making vows to never be like Dad the worrier or Mom the overspender. In either case, we are not free to develop a relationship with money that reflects our own inner values and our own sense of integrity.

Adopting or Rejecting Our Parents' Money Styles

I can give you a good example of what I mean by adopting our parents' money styles by telling you about my own experiences. My father tended to worry about money a lot—too much, in my opinion. My mother, who suffered from feelings of loneliness and low self-esteem, tried to fill up her inner emptiness by buying herself clothing. She went shopping not only when she was lonely or depressed but when she felt like celebrating. My mother didn't work outside the home in those years when I was growing up, and she must have felt guilty about those out-of-control shopping binges. So she would come home and hide the clothes behind the living room chair till my dad was in a good mood and then try them on in front of him, slowly integrating the items into her wardrobe. I thought this ritual was a little ridiculous, and I was upset that my mother's main way of expressing love to me was through buying me clothes. But—to my amazement—when I was grown up and married to a man who was earning about the same income as I was, I found myself alternating between my dad's worrying about money and my mom's shopaholism. In fact, I would even symbolically hide the clothes behind the living room chair till my husband was in a good mood; yet it was my own money I was spending, and most of the clothes were quite reasonably priced! I was careening back and forth between my parents' money modes with no awareness of these dynamics—until I started doing money awareness work with others.

Irma, on the other hand, was a client of mine who rejected her father's powerful money style. Her father, like mine, was deeply affected by the Great Depression. As a result, he was an extreme hoarder and worrier, who used to make Irma account for every penny of her allowance in a weekly ritual she found humiliating and demeaning. She vowed she'd never be a hoarder like her father (so she became an overspender), that she'd never be a worrier (so she avoided dealing with details of her moneylife). Most important, she vowed, "Never again will I let any man control me with money!" So when her husband, Ron, who tended to be a saver, would ask politely for her check register so he could balance their joint checkbook, she would launch into an angry tirade, accusing him of trying to control her as her dad had.

It took only a few minutes of money awareness talk with Irma for her to see that her husband was *not* her father, and to find a good way of giving Ron the information he needed without opening up her old wound. By working with Irma and other clients who had troubled relationships with money, I began to get a handle on my own shopaholic tendencies and started to take steps toward changing them. When I realized how ludicrous it was for me to be aping my mother in hiding my own clothing purchases behind the living room chair, I was able to stop this unconscious practice and to confide in my husband about my struggles around shopping. A little bit of awareness about our money messages and vows from childhood can go a long way in helping us cast off our old, automatic responses to money that are not serving us well as adults.

How was money handled by your relatives when you were growing up? You may want to write down your memories and responses, or tape-record them—or just think about this aspect of your money history. Here are some questions to help you get started:

Money Memories About Family Members and Other Relatives

❧ What are your impressions of how your mother dealt with money? How did she feel about money? How did she feel about her work (either in or out of the house)? How did she feel about your father and how he dealt with money? What interactions do you remember between you and your mother concerning money?

❧ What do you remember about your father and his attitudes toward money? How did he handle his money? How did he feel about his work and about how much money he made? How did he feel about your mother and her way of dealing with money? Do you remember any interactions between you and your father about money? Between your mother and father? What thoughts or feelings do you have about these interactions?

❧ If you have siblings, did your parents treat you all the same when it came to money, or were there differences? How did this treatment affect you? What are your siblings' attitudes toward money now? How do you understand differences between their attitudes and your own?

❧ Did any other relatives (grandparents, godfathers, godmothers, aunts, uncles, cousins, etc.) influence the way you think about money today? If so, what specific messages did you get from each of them? How might these messages be affecting you today?

The Family's Financial Circumstances

Most of the time, direct and open communication about the family's finances just doesn't happen. What does get communicated is free-floating anxiety, fear, and a general sense of malaise. This causes a lot of psychic harm and can lead to intense anxiety, whether there is any reason for worry or not.

Leonard's story, which I heard

while appearing on a radio show, is the most powerful example I
can think of to illustrate this point. I was talking about the importance of revisiting childhood traumas about money when we are
adults, for by this stage in our life we have developed the maturity
to finally exorcise these demons. The fifty-six-year-old Leonard
called in with his own amazing tale. "When I was a teenager," he
said, "I worked in my mother's restaurant, and she was always
talking about how we were on the brink of financial catastrophe. I
had so much anxiety about this that I developed a stammer, and I
worked day and night, even on weekends, to help us stay afloat.
Years later, my mother was in my living room, talking about the
good old days when we were making so much money in the restaurant business! I lost control and started screaming at her about all
the time I spent worrying about our money and all the anxiety I
carried that was not even based on a real financial threat or crisis!
I've never yelled at my mother like that before or since, and when
I had finished my tirade, I noticed, to my amazement, that my
stammer was gone and it never came back!"

Leonard's story is a therapist's dream: one catharsis, and a
complete resolution of symptoms! But even if your own tale is less
dramatic, you may remember living with severe misimpressions
about your family's financial status—or with no knowledge about
it at all. Now is a good time to think about such memories.

* Did either parent (or anybody else) give you any specific information about the financial status of your family? Did you have a sense
of whether you were poor, comfortable, wealthy, or whether your
family's fortunes fluctuated? If you did have this information, how
did you react to it? Is there some way in which this knowledge, or
lack thereof, is still affecting you today?

* Did you ever feel guilty or ashamed about how much or how little
money you thought your family had, as compared with others around
you?

§ Did either parent worry about money? If so, was it your mother or your father—or perhaps both parents? Was the worrying done out loud or silently and covertly? If your parent(s) did worry or act anxious about money, what effect did this have on you?

§ Did you ever feel as if there was some sort of financial problem in your family, but you had no idea what it was? If so, can you remember how this perception affected you at the time? Did you ever find out about any money secrets that your parents had kept from you? If so, what was your reaction?

§ Did you ever discover that you had a totally inaccurate picture of the family's economic status while growing up? If so, how and when did you learn the truth, and what was your reaction? Can you now see how this inaccurate picture affected your life, both in the past and in the present?

Sometimes, a child's ignorance about the family's finances causes a problem for the *parent*. Consider what happened to Henry, whose two teenage children were constantly asking him for money and attacking him when he said he didn't make enough to give them any more. He felt under so much stress that he sought the help of a budget counselor at the navy base where he was stationed. The counselor restored Henry's confidence in his ability to handle his money and told him a simple way to solve the problem with his children. She urged him to take out his next paycheck in one-dollar bills, to have a family money meeting around the kitchen table, and to count out every bill he had to pay in front of his teenagers. Henry took the counselor's suggestion and came back to see her the next week, smiling from ear to ear. "You won't believe what happened," he said. "Both my thirteen-year-old and my fifteen-year-old actually apologized for giving me such a hard time and offered to find part-time work to help out." This turnabout occurred only because Henry gave his children concrete information about the family's financial circumstances.

What works with teenagers might very well be a waste of time with much younger children. The point is that when parents are not afraid to give their children a clear, objective, and age-appropriate picture of the family's finances, the two generations are more likely to become allies rather than adversaries.

From my clients and workshop participants, I have learned that there are a variety of ways in which allowances are dealt with in the family and that how allowances are handled can have profound effects on the children. Some people recalled that they never had an allowance and so never learned to deal with money at all until they were  adults. Some of these individuals said that as children they got whatever they wanted from their parents and developed the belief that the money would always be there when they needed it. When they were grown, they were shocked to learn that this wasn't true. Others were given allowances but were not allowed to spend the money on candy or certain toys. This stipulation made them feel that their money was never really their own and caused them to harbor resentment toward their parents, especially when they saw that their friends could spend their allowances on whatever they wanted. Some clients felt that if their parents dictated how they spent their allowance, they (the children) couldn't be trusted to make good choices about money. In some cases, these people were still telling themselves that they were not to be trusted about money when they became adults. Others were paid for getting *A*s on their report cards. They reported that this practice made them feel that the only reason for working hard is to get money, and they didn't like the way it increased the pressure on them to excel. Others were paid for chores and said that in later years, when they were part of a family, their spouses complained they never helped around the house. They reflected that they probably were still waiting to be paid for their services!

Let's now take a look at your own experience—or lack of experience—as far as allowances are concerned.

    ✒ How were allowances dealt with in your family? Did you have one? Was it given to you consistently or on and off?

    ✒ If you got an allowance, how old were you when this practice began? How much did you get? Was it more or less than other peers got?

    ✒ Was your allowance taken away as a punishment? If so, as a punishment for what?

    ✒ Were you asked to account for how you spent your allowance, or were you free to do with it as you wished?

    ✒ How did you feel about all of this? What conclusions might you have drawn about what money meant from the way allowances were handled in your family?

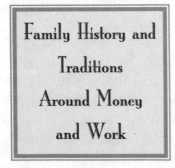

Family History and Traditions Around Money and Work

Ken came to me for therapy because he was experiencing extreme anxiety attacks in graduate school, where he was an art student. Not only was he the first to get a college degree in his working-class family, but there were no artists before him. He didn't fully realize until coming to therapy that what he was feeling was a kind of "survivor guilt" because his own father had had to leave college in order to support a family. After several months in therapy, Ken started feeling more pride in his career choice, more confidence in listening to his own inner voice, and better able to dialogue with his family about this courageous path he had chosen. Ken wanted to get his father's blessing to pursue his dream. Although not all fathers would be willing to extend themselves in this way, Ken could eventually ask his father for what he needed and get it. This support, of course, helped Ken joyfully embrace his career as an artist.

Whereas Ken was departing from family tradition, you may well be continuing a tradition (such as running the family business or being a third-generation teacher). Or perhaps you find yourself following in the footsteps of one or more members of your family who are particularly successful (your father the wealthy doctor, or your mother the crackerjack businesswoman, or your older sister who has distinguished herself in the military). Let's take a closer look.

* Are you continuing a tradition of your family when it comes to work and money? The use of money? Philanthropy? Does adhering to this tradition work for you? If not, what changes would you like to make? What is preventing you from making these changes?

* Are there supposedly positive models from your childhood that seem like a burden to you today? Do you feel a pressure to be as successful or wealthy as certain family members? Do you feel pressured to pursue a similar field, or to make sure you avoid that field at all costs because of the threat of comparison? Would you like to change your reactions to these successes in your family? If so, in what way?

* Are there family traditions about money, work, spending, saving, and/or investing that you are departing from? How do you feel about

departing from these historical patterns? Do you feel proud, guilty, ashamed, or a combination of all of these feelings? How would you like to feel about being a pioneer in this way?

Money Messages

from

Your Religious

Training

In some cases, religious training in childhood communicates powerful messages about money and its meanings. Some workshop participants tell me that in their religious schools they learned that "money is the root of all evil." (The Bible actually says "Love of money is the root of all evil," cautioning against greed and not against money per se.) This message might well leave a person afraid of making too much money, or inheriting too much money, for fear it will corrupt him or her.

Take some time to ask yourself these questions:

🖝 Are there any messages you learned from your religious training in childhood that relate to money and its use? If so, how did you react to these messages? How might this religious training around money be affecting you today?

🖝 Are you abandoning any religious messages you received in your childhood about money? How does this make you feel?

🖝 Was there any conflict between messages you got from your religious training and messages you got, either overtly or covertly, from your family or from society? If so, is this conflict still alive in you today? How does it manifest itself? What would you like to do about it?

Our peers can exert a strong influence on our lives, especially during our formative years. When it comes to money, we often compare ourselves with our peers in terms of financial status and habits.

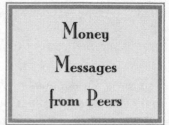

Money Messages from Peers

In thinking back, you may remember being much poorer—or richer—than the rest of the kids in your classes. Perhaps you had a friend who would rather spend money on designer clothes than on lunch, and another who worked a part-time job to help with the family finances. You might have had a friend who made a practice of borrowing money without paying it back. Consider the messages your peers were sending out and how you reacted.

- Were any of your peers much richer or poorer than you, and how did this affect your attitude toward money and your way of handling your money?
- When you were around your peers, did you feel shame, pride, guilt, envy, or fear around money?
- Do you remember specific incidents connected with your peers and money that are still in your mind today? What emotions do these memories evoke? How might they be affecting you now?

In some cases, our most emotional memories about money from childhood may not come from anyone close to us. Sometimes, there are incidents or events that happen to us, or around us, that leave such a powerful impression that we make money vows which we

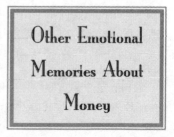

Other Emotional Memories About Money

carry well into adulthood. I have one such indelible memory from when I was extremely young—about five or six years old. I remember this incident, and the feelings surrounding it, as if it were yesterday.

I was in a barbershop with my dad, and I remember watching a young boy, probably around seven years old, beg his father for a quarter. His dad refused him coldly, and the little boy started to sob. I felt gripped by his anguish and sense of deprivation as I witnessed this upsetting scene. So I made a vow that I would *never* feel as deprived as that child did. I firmly believe that this vow contributed heavily to my overspending tendencies; whether I had the money or not, I would act as if I did. Since becoming aware of this and other money vows, I have been calling myself a "recovering overspender." My tendency to deny any sense of deprivation is losing its grip on my psyche and on my spending behavior.

Money Messages from Society

Sometimes the most profound influence on us in our growing-up years comes from society at large—through the media (books, newspapers, TV) and ingrained cultural beliefs. Since the advent of television and the explosion in advertising on every level, we have been bombarded by messages that tell us the key to happiness is to buy everything you could ever imagine needing or wanting. Ads encouraging us to "keep up with the Joneses"—or better yet, to surpass them—are everywhere. And this conditioning may well have started for most of us when we were very young.

When my son was in first grade, he had to write an essay on what he would do if he found a pot of gold at the end of the rainbow. (The very assignment sends some questionable messages that promote the desirability of instant wealth and the possibility of getting something for nothing.) Many of the kids in the class wrote about buying toys and candy. But my son, affected by the money messages he was receiving from TV shows and commercials as well as by his best friend who had an older brother influencing him, wrote an essay about buying a mansion, a Jaguar *and* a Lamborghini, and other luxury items. At the time, I didn't even know what a Lamborghini was, and I was never particularly interested in expensive cars, so I know he didn't get this idea from me! In fact, none of the parental influences in my boy's life explains why he asked whether hotels have Jacuzzis and expressed similar appetites for the good life in general. I believe it was mainly the influences of TV and his first-grade buddy that encouraged him on this track.

It is important to remember that the people and events in our past did not just constitute negative influences. Either consciously or unconsciously, we've picked up positive attitudes and behaviors from them. Remembering the positive as well as the negative is  essential in this process of self-exploration. So ask yourself the following questions:

   ✹ What positive money models do you have in your past? Are they your parents? Other relatives? Religious teachers? Peers? Other people you knew or read about?

   ✹ What events in your childhood shaped your relationship with money in a positive way?

   ✹ What specific money skills and attitudes did these positive influences provide you with? Have you incorporated these skills and attitudes into your adult life as much as you'd like, or do you want to do more in this regard?

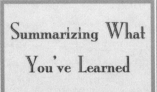

Since we have covered a lot of ground in this chapter, I think it's a good idea for you to summarize what you've learned. Ask yourself:

✺ What messages did you get from your family, friends, religious training, as well as society at large, that still affect your relationship with money?

✺ Do you have any emotional or traumatic memories around money, independent of family, religious, and peer influences, that may be affecting you today?

✺ What childhood vows did you make that may be controlling you in your life with money today?

✺ What positive influences from the past would you like to preserve?

✺ What changes would you like to make in your present life so that it is less affected by the past?

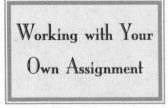

In the next week or so, take one action designed to help you feel freer from past influences in your handling of money. (For example, if you're a carbon copy of your mother in your hoarding behavior, you might decide to purchase a nonessential item such as an article of clothing.) Make sure to give yourself a reward for taking this action. Choose a reward that does not reinforce any of your negative ways of handling money; instead, select something that increases your sense of self-esteem. Remember to notice your reactions to this new behavior. If you're willing, write down or tape-record these responses.

You may find, after doing all this good self-awareness work, that your negative patterns around money will temporarily intensify, instead of abating. Don't be too upset by relapses into old, dysfunctional habits. When we confront our demons, and try to tame them, they often rear their ugly heads with more energy than usual. Moreover, growth 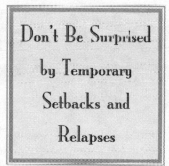 and change usually occur in a process that is one step forward, one-half step back. Relapses are normal and should be greeted with patience and understanding. If you do not panic, your greater self-awareness and commitment to try on new attitudes and actions will keep you moving in a forward direction.

3.

Money Myths: Learning to

Identify and Debunk Them

W hat are money myths? Money myths are global beliefs about all the wonderful, almost magical things that money can do for us. Though each of these myths contains some modicum of truth, taking them as gospel can prevent us from making rational decisions with our money. Most Americans believe in *at least* one money myth; many of us believe in a number of them. These beliefs can trigger intense emotions about money (anxiety, fear, obsession) and can even make it difficult for us to handle the simplest financial decisions and tasks.

Here are the most common money myths:

Money = Happiness   Money = Freedom
Money = Love   Money = Self-worth
Money = Power   Money = Security

What do we need to do about these money myths? First we must identify the myths that are affecting us personally. Next we must spend some time debunking the money myths, one by one. Only then will we be free to use money and make decisions about our money in a way that enhances our life rather than constrains it.

Money equals happiness is one of the most prevalent myths in our culture. We are raised on stories about people who worked hard, struck it rich, and lived happily ever after. Such individuals as Horatio Alger, Andrew Carnegie, and lately Donald Trump, Oprah Winfrey, Ted Turner, and Jane Fonda, serve as the quintessential models of success. But do we really know enough about these men and women to know if they are truly happy and whether money is the primary factor in their supposed happiness?

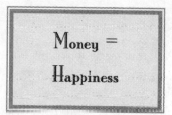

Even our old tired jokes reflect this pervasive belief that money equals happiness. Consider these common sayings: "Being rich isn't everything, but it sure beats whatever is in second place!" "I've been rich and I've been poor, and rich is better." In an old musical from the 1940s called *Allegro*, there's a song called "Money Isn't Everything." It uses sarcasm to describe all the "wonderful" things that money cannot do (e.g., "it cannot . . . teach you how to starve") and ends with the line "Money isn't everything, except when you are poor." So the point of the song is that money might not be everything, but it is certainly central to our happiness.

Of course, being poor or financially stressed definitely *does* affect our happiness. But it is not the prime determinant of our happiness and satisfaction in life, and we would do well to remember that. Otherwise, we will be driven to amass large sums of money in a way that may well impinge on or even destroy the happiness we hoped money would create.

DO YOU BELIEVE THAT MONEY = HAPPINESS?

If you want to know for sure whether you believe in the money-equals-happiness myth, ask yourself the following questions:

- Do you tend to believe that money leads to happiness, fulfillment, contentment?

- Do you catch yourself thinking, "If only I had (made) a little more money (or a lot more money), everything would be great"?

- Do you envy others who make more money than you do, or who have more money or more things, assuming that they must be happier than you are because of their greater financial ease?

- When you encounter someone who you know is not very wealthy, do you assume that the person couldn't really be happy?

- Would having to take a small decrease in your own or your partner's income make you feel very upset?

If you answered yes to at least three of these five questions, you are influenced by the money-equals-happiness myth.

DEBUNKING MONEY =
HAPPINESS

To begin to challenge this belief, I recommend that you think
about, write down, or tape-record the answers to the following
three questions:

* What two activities do you love to do that make you very happy?

* How much does it cost to do these activities?

* Are these activities best done alone or with others?

I have done this exercise with many diverse groups through the
years. Invariably, the majority of people in each group will choose
at least one activity that costs very little money or no money at all.
(For most people, making love is on the free list!) And most people
find that at least one of their activities, if not both, is best done
with another person. So maybe it is social connections that equals
happiness. Participants in my workshops are pleasantly surprised
when they realize that many of the things they love in their lives
cost nothing or next to nothing. If your results are similar, let this
awareness remind you that much of your happiness has very little
to do with money at all.

Here is another useful exercise you might try:

* For one week or one month, keep track of what you spend your
  money on.

* On a scale of 1 to 10, rate the fulfillment that each expenditure
  brings you.

This exercise can be a real eye-opener, for it shows you many
ways in which you use your money that don't add one iota to your
happiness and fulfillment.

If, after reading and trying these exercises, you still believe that "if only I had a little more money (or a lot more money), I would *really* be happy," take a little time to search for and note examples that run counter to the money-equals-happiness myth. Think about people you know personally, or have read or heard about, who:

* Don't have a lot of money but are very happy.
* Have a lot of money and are not happy.

When I was a guest on a TV talk show in 1991, I met Dennis, an earnest man who had just won the lottery. He shared with me his feelings of unhappiness and anxiety after this supposedly wonderful event brought him a large amount of money. Dennis had had dozens of business proposals—and even a few marriage proposals from women he didn't know! He had become mistrustful: How could he possibly distinguish between those who were reacting to his money and those who were responding to him as an individual? This windfall made Dennis's life a living hell for a while. And even though he was learning how to deal with his situation, he would never say that for him, money equaled happiness. In fact, many other lottery winners also report that the vast change in their financial status has had a very destabilizing effect on their lives and has created more problems than it solved.

Here is a final assignment for those of you who feel affected or controlled by this money myth:

* Every day for a week spend time on activities, old or new, that cost little or nothing and that bring you happiness.

* Notice and record your feelings about each of these activities. Doing this assignment will help you realize that there is much in your life (or there could be) that costs little and makes you happy.

You may also be heartened by the testimony of readers of a magazine called *The Sun*, who wrote in on the subject of "wealth."* Many of their letters said, in essence, "When I think back on the last twenty years, I realize that my husband [or my wife] and I were happiest when we were making less money. Our lives were simpler; we were more creative about doing things we wanted to do; we were less workaholic; and we had more time and energy to enjoy life and each other. That seemed like true wealth to us."

In these recessionary times, with so much real financial uncertainty in the air, freeing yourself from the belief that money equals happiness can enable you to better roll with the punches. If you are denied a cost-of-living increase or a raise because of tough financial times at your job, you will tend to feel less depressed and deprived. Whatever the financial ups and downs, you'll stand a much better chance of getting enjoyment out of life.

Every time we turn on our TV, we are bombarded with commercials that try to link money with love in our minds. They tell us that if we would just buy this flower-fresh deodorant, or that new and improved shampoo, or the latest

> **Money = Love**

model of that snazzy sports car, we'd have all the love and happiness we could want. Advertisements in newspapers and magazines are sending us the same messages. This dangerous cultural conditioning, and the "keeping up with the Joneses" mentality that fuels it, contributes to the epidemic of compulsive spending in this coun-

* This fascinating collection of letters appeared in April 1989, in a section entitled "Readers on Wealth." It was startling to see how many of the letters did not equate real wealth, and the feeling of abundance that comes from deep fulfillment, with financial wealth.

try. Many of us believe not only that money equals love but that money can substitute for a *lack* of love.

DO YOU BELIEVE THAT
MONEY = LOVE?

To find out if you are among the many who believe in the myth that money equals love, answer the following questions:

- When you feel lonely or depressed, do you buy yourself something to cheer yourself up?

- Do you tend to buy yourself something as a way of celebrating or rewarding yourself for a job well done?

- Do you tend to shop impulsively or compulsively?

- Do you buy things for yourself or others regardless of whether you have enough money to pay for these purchases?

- When you feel deprived or unloved, does buying yourself something seem like the first recourse?

If you answered yes to three or more of these questions, then money equals love for you, at least to some extent.

DEBUNKING MONEY = LOVE

If you subscribe to this myth in your actions and attitudes, you may need to spend some time thinking about people you know personally who:

* Don't have a lot of money but have a lot of love in their life.
* Have a lot of money but seem starved for love.

The next step in debunking this myth is to practice new ways of nurturing yourself that don't cost much money (or perhaps cost no money at all). If you tend to reward yourself by shopping (impulsively or compulsively), think of alternate activities that would serve the same purpose. For example, you might take a hot bath or have a long talk with your best friend. You could attend a religious service, listen to music, read a book, meditate, make love, or go to a museum. The possibilities are endless!

If you feel that the urge to shop comes over you like a tidal wave, and that you can't say no to it, you may well have a spending addiction. There's no need to be ashamed about this problem. You are far from alone. Its source is usually a combination of early childhood deprivation (on an emotional, physical, or material level) as well as the social alienation that comes from being in a culture where there is a lack of community, a feeling of spiritual emptiness, and a craving to feel whole on some level. The only problem with the solution of using money as a substitute for love is that it doesn't work. It is like a Band-Aid on a festering wound, providing temporary relief from the feelings of loneliness, pain, or emptiness, but never actually healing the wound. In fact, these "quick fixes" erode self-esteem over time and create a self-perpetuating downward spiral that can often lead to more severe emotional as well as financial crises.

If you do think that you spend in a way that feels like a compulsion or addiction, a twelve-step program such as Debtors Anonymous, which costs nothing, can offer invaluable group support and concrete help in resolving this problem. Members often choose to join "pressure groups" in DA, which can help them make better decisions about their money, as well as enhance their self-esteem and provide emotional support. There are over 400 branches in forty-one states. (Appendix B provides more information on this organization.)

Money = Power

The myth that money equals power is deeply entrenched in the media. Advertisements, especially car ads, are adept at communicating this "truth." TV programs and movies, such as *Wall Street* and *Pretty Woman*, show us rich men who control the world in exciting ways. They also demonstrate the flip side of this myth: that money equals power in an evil sense, and that these rich people will end up destroying their lives or the lives of others with all their money.

As I said earlier, some truth is contained in every money myth. When we look around us, we see not just fictional but real-life examples of wealthy people who use their money and the status that may accompany it to wield power over others. It's been said that for many women, power is a great aphrodisiac; and wealthy men have often had an advantage in seducing and coupling with women. Many of us have had personal experience with superiors at work, who make more money and have more power than we do, using their authority over us in ways that constrain us and make us feel powerless. Having money can lead to more choices (of educational and job training, for example) and can enable us to travel far and wide and to procure many of the things we want. It can buy good health care. And of course, all of these things are a kind of power.

But debunking the myth that money equals power can lead to new, creative life choices for us and our intimates.

DO YOU BELIEVE THAT
MONEY = POWER?

To see if you believe in this money myth, ask yourself which of the
following statements seem true to you:

- The most powerful people in the world are rich.
- If I had more money, I'd definitely be more powerful.
- When people lose money, they lose power.
- I need a lot of money to accomplish my goals and feel in control
  of my life.
- Less money means less power to live my life as I choose.

If you agree with three or more of these statements, the money-
equals-power myth seems at least partially true to you.

DEBUNKING MONEY = POWER

If you think that money equals power in a *positive* sense (power to
get what you want and need in life), then think about, write down,
or tape-record your impressions of a few people you know personally, or have read or heard about, who:

- Don't have a lot of money but seem quite powerful to you.
- Have a lot of money but lack personal power.

Now consider:

- What factors (besides money) are necessary in attaining personal
power (power to build a fulfilling life, accomplish one's life goals,
maintain fulfilling relationships, etc.)?

- On a scale of 1 to 10, how would you rate the importance of money
and these other factors in attaining these desired goals?

When I think of people who are not wealthy and have tremendous personal power, the first examples who come to mind are famous people who have changed the world in some sense. (For me, that is the height of personal power.) Mother Teresa, who refuses large donations of money and seeks personal help and support, has nurtured thousands of abandoned children; and Ralph Nader, who is famous for following a spartan lifestyle, has been working to make our society a better place for consumers.

If you believe, on the other hand, that money equals power in a *negative* sense (power to corrupt and destroy lives), then you need to find examples of people you know personally, or have read or heard about, who:

- Have a lot of money and use it not to wield negative power but to enhance their lives and the lives of others.
- Don't have a lot of money but wield power in a negative way.

When I think about people who have a lot of money and use it well, I think about entertainers who sponsor benefits like Live Aid, Comic Relief, and Farm Aid; Elizabeth Taylor and her work raising money to combat AIDS; and families such as the MacArthurs, who give grants to reward geniuses for their creative endeavors and to allow them to pursue their work less encumbered by financial constraints. I also think of Ben Cohen (of Ben and Jerry's ice cream), who organizes his business and uses his money to promote world peace, shared profit in business, and more egalitarian models of leadership.* There are numerous other examples of people who use their wealth to enhance the lives of others.

* Ben Cohen's remarkable journey through the business world and his enlightened business practices are chronicled in *We Gave Away a Fortune: Stories of People Who Have Devoted Themselves and Their Wealth to Peace, Justice, and a Healthy Environment*, by Christopher Mogil and Anne Slepian, with Peter Woodrow (Philadelphia: New Society Publishers, 1992), pp. 91–94.

But remember that money cannot buy personal fulfillment, and the power that comes from being truly in harmony with your own values and living out a life that you love and respect. Money cannot buy spiritual fulfillment; it cannot buy friendship. When we look around and see examples of those who thought they had tremendous financial power but then lost it, people like Leona Helmsley and Ivan Boesky, we realize that the heady wine of power through money may not ultimately be as satisfying as many of us think. It's not uncommon for people making huge amounts of money to be workaholics who sacrifice health and personal relationships for the power they think money will bring. So, in the end, what constitutes true power for us? Is it power over others or, as Warren Farrell defines it, "control over our own lives"?* And aren't there many ways to achieve control over our own lives that are not determined by money?

Let's apply the idea of achieving personal power to your own life.

* In what areas of your life would you want to feel personally powerful?

* Is money involved in the attainment of all these goals, some of these goals, or none of these goals? If so, how much money?

* What adjectives would best describe how you would feel about achieving personal power in your own life?

* Warren Farrell, *Why Men Are the Way They Are: The Male-Female Dynamic* (New York: Berkley Books, 1988), pp. 9–12. Farrell has spent many years of his life exploring numerous aspects of power and powerlessness in our culture. He has tried to help both men and women deal with their own powerlessness without blaming each other for their situation, so that the two sexes can achieve real control over their own lives instead of power over each other.

Money = Freedom

Money equals freedom is a myth that many of us hold dear. As long as we secretly, or not so secretly, cling to this one, we never have to ask ourselves what we really want to do with our lives, and what might be preventing us from doing it. We can comfortably tell ourselves, "If only I had more money, I would be free to paint; write that novel; travel to Europe; change professions . . . to do what I really want to do or what I was meant to do." And, of course, since doing some of the things we want to do in fact *does* cost money, the partial truth of this myth makes it convenient for us to hold on to it, instead of challenging the notion and perhaps achieving real freedom.

DO YOU BELIEVE THAT MONEY = FREEDOM?

If you think you may be controlled by this myth, determine whether you agree with the following statements:

- Having more money would enable me to do what I really want to do in my life.
- It is mainly money that is preventing me from doing what I really want to do.
- Wealthy people are truly freer to create the kind of life they want.
- The key to real freedom is to have enough money.
- I often think wistfully about all the things I could do, and all the freedom I would have, if only I had more money.

If you answered "true" to three or more of these statements, money equals freedom to you, at least to some degree.

DEBUNKING MONEY =
FREEDOM

If you believe that money equals freedom, here's an exercise you can do to begin challenging this notion. Identify and describe, in as much detail as possible, a few people you know personally, or have read or heard about, who:

- Don't have a lot of money but seem very free to you.
- Have a lot of money but don't seem to be free at all.

Figuring out what constitutes true freedom is the work of a lifetime. But I don't believe that money is the major determinant—as long as we have enough to meet our basic needs and wants, for food, shelter, clothing, and for some pleasures of life that do cost money.

Speaking of pleasures, let's focus for a moment on travel. Recently, a wise old friend of mine named Richard made some astute observations on the connection between money and the freedom to travel. He described the experiences of friends of his who had gone to Europe on a shoestring many years ago. They hitchhiked around, stayed in small villages as guests in the homes of people they met while traveling. They really got a sense of what each culture was like. He contrasted them to people he knew who were rich and wanted to go to Europe but who felt they had to stay home and make sure their money was growing. He also mentioned those who went to foreign countries and stayed in ritzy American-style hotels, never getting out and seeing the people and experiencing these cultures. To him, that didn't seem like freedom at all.

Of course, freedom is a tricky notion. We are not talking about freedom to act out all our impulses, however destructive. No amount of wealth makes this freedom permissible. We *are* talking about the freedom to do all that we wish to do, and to be all that we wish to be.

Let's now turn to an exercise that you might find useful in debunking the myth that money equals freedom:

- For one week or one month, keep track of what you spend your money on.
- On a scale of 1 to 10, rate how much pleasure each expenditure brings you.
- Note how much time you have to spend working to make the money to pay for these expenditures.

This process can be revealing, for it may point up ways that you are giving up your freedom and free time to purchase things you do not value or enjoy very much.

If you are willing to take a positive step in moving closer to your dreams and goals, think about the following:

- What could you do in the next six months that would give you more freedom without requiring a major change in your financial situation?
- What has prevented you from doing this thus far? Is it really money or something else?
- How could you do this, or take a step toward doing it, in the next week, couple of weeks, or month?

If you do take this action, remember to reward yourself and to monitor your thoughts and feelings (in writing, on tape, or at least in your mind) about moving in the direction of real freedom.

The myth of money equals self-worth comes up for many men and women when they're thinking about how much they are paid for the work they do. As a self-employed psychotherapist, I used to say to myself, "I'm trying to set a fee

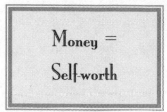

Money =
Self-worth

for my services, but how much am I worth?" My therapist col leagues in private practice are often heard asking themselves and one another the same question in those exact words. Now it makes me cringe a little to realize how quickly we all equated our self-worth with the amount of money we charged for our work. Perhaps a more appropriate question to ask, if you are self-employed, is one of the following: "What's the going rate?" "What's a fair amount to charge?" "How much do I need to make?" "How much feels right for me to charge?" or even "How much can I tolerate charging without feeling guilty or having an anxiety attack?"

Men are, of course, socialized in our culture to equate self-worth with success in work; women historically tend to rate themselves more according to success in intimate relationships. But as increasing numbers of women have entered the workforce in higher-level positions, they are becoming more and more susceptible to measuring their self-worth by the amount of money they make. So this equation of money with self-worth has become a serious problem for both sexes.

DO YOU BELIEVE THAT
MONEY = SELF-WORTH?

If you think that you subscribe to this myth, ask yourself the following questions:

* Do you feel a lot better about yourself when you're making more money?
* Does the income of people close to you affect how much you respect them?
* Do you fear that people would look down on you if you underwent a salary cut, for any reason?
* Would being unemployed for a short period make you feel bad about yourself?
* Do you lose some respect for people if you find out that they are making much less money than you thought they were?

If you answered yes to three or more questions, then to some degree you believe that money equals self-worth.

DEBUNKING MONEY = SELF-WORTH

If you believe that your self-worth is tied to money, you need to look for examples that run counter to this powerful myth. Identify and describe, in as much detail as possible, a few people you know personally, or have read or heard about, who:

* Don't have a lot of money but, in your opinion, have an abundance of self-esteem.
* Have a lot of money but seem to have very little sense of self-worth.

The next exercise for debunking this myth is as follows:

* Imagine something you could be doing with your life that would not involve a lot of money but that would enhance your self-esteem or sense of self-worth.

* Write down a description of this activity or situation.

Bear in mind that for the time being you are under *no* pressure to take action; just imagine this scenario. At some future time, you may want to take a concrete step toward your goal.

If you lose your job suddenly, it is in your best interest to discard the belief that money equals self-worth as quickly as possible. Tina's story will illustrate what I mean by this statement. Recently, she came to me for therapy after receiving notice that she was being laid off at work. Though she admitted that the job she held had been unsatisfying for the last two years, and that in her heart she knew it was time to move on, she was reeling from the shock of being laid off with two weeks' notice. She was doubting her abilities and feeling shaken in her self-esteem because her salary was removed abruptly and she was soon to be out of work. It took only a few sessions to help Tina disconnect her feelings of self-worth from this work trauma and start to reconnect with her real sense of energy and passion in work. Within a month, she was volunteering in a field she loved but had not had time to pursue. Within three months, she had been offered a position in that new, more creative arena. The beginning salary was slightly lower than that in her old job, but she felt no decrease in self-esteem. Quite the contrary: Working in an area she loved increased her confidence and zest for life.

Since none of us had perfect parents, we go through life with holes in our psyches. We try to fill in the gaps through our jobs (as in Tina's case), our other achievements, our possessions, and, for some of us, by trying to make more and more money. But I believe the only way of truly enhancing our self-esteem and self-worth is to keep on working to fulfill more and more of our potential: to strive to be the best we can be in the areas of our life in which we feel passion and commitment. If we attach self-worth to the vagaries of the financial marketplace, we will be standing on shaky ground indeed. And the temporary admiration of others at our financial success can never fill us up over time in the same way that our own self-love and self-respect will.

| Money = Security |

Money equals security is a very prevalent myth in our society, even though we tend to be a society of spenders rather than savers. Who among us does not believe, to a certain extent, that money is one of the main things that will provide us with some security, especially in our old age? This money myth, like all the others, contains some kernel of truth. We do need enough financial security to make us feel at ease about our ability to take care of ourselves and our loved ones. But believing this money myth and investing too much emotional energy in it can be potentially destructive and even paralyzing.

Take David, for example. His uncle had gone bankrupt as a result of a bad business deal and had attempted suicide. This financial tragedy had such a profound effect on David's dad that he worried all the time about not having enough money and lectured his children about the evils of frivolous spending. David grew up to be a lawyer who worked day and night to make money. He had an intense drive to save more and more money for his retirement years so he and his wife could live comfortably and still provide their three kids with a substantial inheritance. David was so worried about not having enough money that he never wanted to take even two weeks off at a time for vacations. He missed his daughter's sixth-grade concert and his son's eighth-grade play because he had to work both nights "to ensure his family's security," as he put it. He attacked his wife for buying a new living room couch when the old one was threadbare, calling this purchase an "unnecessary luxury." At the age of forty-eight, he had the first of two heart attacks. With all this money, David was not secure. And if he died early, his children, the youngest of whom was six when the first heart attack struck, would not feel very secure and safe, even with more than enough money.

DO YOU BELIEVE THAT MONEY = SECURITY?

To see whether this money myth has a grip on you, ask yourself the following questions:

* When you think about *not* having a lot of money saved for the future, do you feel very uneasy and insecure?

* Do you judge people who spend a lot of money for present pleasures and short-term goals as being unwise and shortsighted?

* When you think about being secure in your old age, is having enough money the first thing (or the main thing) that comes to mind?

* Does putting money away in savings or in other "safe" investments give you a feeling of inner peace and security more than any other action does?

* If you have fears about your old age, does thinking about having more than enough money during that period comfort you and allay most of your fears?

If you answered yes to three or more of these questions, you probably believe that money equals security.

DEBUNKING MONEY =
SECURITY

The trick in debunking this myth is to find a few examples that serve to contradict it. So I suggest that you identify and describe, in as much detail as possible, some elderly people you know who:

- Don't have a lot of money but seem very secure to you.
- Have a lot of money but don't seem at all secure.

What do you think is the difference between these people? What does one have that the other doesn't that leads to more real security?

My friend Michael Phillips, author of *The Seven Laws of Money*, *Honest Business*, *Simple Living Investments*, and other books, helped debunk this myth for me personally. He once said to me that when he looked around at the elderly people he knew and tried to determine who seemed truly secure, he found that money was not the determining factor. Of course, he acknowledged, elderly people do need enough money for the basic necessities of life and for some pleasures and luxuries as well. But what distinguished these secure old people from the others was that they were not isolated; they were surrounded by a supportive network of friends of various ages. Goods and services were naturally exchanged in the course of their lives. Their friends were glad to take them grocery shopping or to shop for them; to accompany them to the movies or to invite them to dinner. So the prime ingredient in ensuring one's security in old age is social connectedness and lack of isolation, not money.

Helen serves as an excellent example of what happens when an elderly person lives with wealth but in isolation. Although she resided in a luxurious retirement community in Florida, Helen disliked people and preferred to sit at home all day watching TV and smoking cigarettes. But sometimes she ruefully observed that because she had no friends, she had to *hire* people to take her grocery shopping and to help her with other chores, and she would be completely on her own in a medical emergency. So even with all her money, Helen did not feel secure. When she was taken ill with a slow, debilitating form of cancer, she began to open up to people for the first time in years. She found loving help and support, and when she died, she was not alone and finally seemed at peace.

Granted, we do need to save money for our retirement and/or our later years of life. But if we understand that money is not security, we will lose some of our general anxiety about whether we are squirreling away enough of it. Instead, we'll be able to redirect some of this energy toward developing more satisfying and lasting personal contacts and friendships.

You are now ready to take a collective look at all the money myths that have had an impact on your life. Consider:

Assessing All the Money Myths in Your Life

* What are your most prevalent money myths?

* How have they been influencing your life?

* How have they affected your love relationships and your relationships in general?

* How would you like to modify these beliefs and the attitudes and behaviors that stem from them?

❋ What can you do, or what do you need to think about or tell yourself, to continue debunking the myths that prevent you from making
rational decisions about your money?

Money does not equal happiness, love, power, freedom, self-
worth, or security. Money equals dollars and cents, and is merely a
tool to facilitate your attaining certain goals and having certain
things. If you remember this, you will not be encumbered by anxiety, guilt, fear, or shame about how to spend, save, or invest your
money. Instead, you'll be able to use your money, both alone and
in relationships, in a rational way that satisfies your real needs and
wants, and that reflects your real values.

4.

Your Money Types: Dealing with

Your Money Personality

In chapter 1, you took and tabulated a quiz that gave you a general idea of which combination of five money personality types you tend to be: hoarder, spender, money monk, avoider, amasser. In this chapter, we'll examine in detail the characteristics of each of these types as well as those of several other money types: binger, worrier, risk taker, and risk avoider.

I've chosen names for the money types that capture the essence of each type quickly and dramatically. Many of my clients have remarked on the negative connotations of the names. Hoarders, for example, have often suggested to me in wounded tones: "Why don't you substitute 'frugal' for 'hoarder'?" The answer is that I want to evoke the tendency toward imbalance in each type. Why? Because if your money type doesn't bother you or others around you, you don't have a problem; as the saying goes, "If it ain't broke, don't fix it." My discussions of each type are designed to help you change the money personality traits that may be causing you trouble, or at least to have more control over them. Thus, I orient my discussion to the weaknesses and problems inherent in each money type.

Remember that *most people are a mixture of types* and do not exemplify only one tendency. It is even possible that in the course of doing your money awareness work, you may change types entirely. And, if you are in a couple relationship, when you join forces with your partner, there may well be a shift to a new money type for one or both of you as you attempt to balance each other out (more about this in chapter 7).

You can, if you choose, read about only the money types that you tend to exemplify. Or you may prefer to read about all of them, to better understand the range of money types you may come into contact with in your life and in your relationships. I will be suggesting specific assignments that fall under the rubric of "doin' what doesn't come naturally." I suggest that you (1) choose your own assignments (either from my suggested list or from your own imagination); (2) record (in writing or on tape) all your thoughts and feelings about practicing actions and attitudes that are at odds with your usual tendencies; and (3) reward yourself for your new behavior (but don't sabotage the process by choosing a reward that reinforces the behavior you wish to change). In this way, you will get the maximum benefit from the chapter.

Hoarder

If you tend to be a hoarder, you like to save money. You also like to prioritize your financial goals. You probably have a budget and may enjoy the processes of making up a budget and reviewing it periodically. You most likely have a hard time spending money on yourself and your loved ones for luxury items or even practical gifts. These purchases would seem frivolous to you. You might very well view spending money on entertainment and on vacations—and even on clothing—as largely unnecessary expenses. If you think about investing your money, you tend to be concerned not with liquidity but with future security, especially during retirement. "Saving for a rainy day" appeals to your orderly nature. If you are an extreme hoarder, you may want to keep your money so close to you that you avoid putting it even in conservative investments such as money markets, bonds, or mutual funds. Some hoarders have been known to keep their money hidden under mattresses and in other secret places rather than put it in a bank. But these cases are relatively rare. Depending on how extreme your hoarder tendencies are, you might exhibit some, most, or all of these traits.

If your hoarding does not feel excessive, or cause you and your loved ones much angst or tension, you may not need to do anything at all about your way of spending—or should I say *not spending*!— money. For you, money may equal security to some degree, but it may work just fine for you in your life. You may, for example, have saved up a substantial amount of money, which will of course provide financial security now and in your later years. But if you sometimes feel too stingy, too worried, or too anxious to enjoy your money in the moment, you may want to consider practicing some new behaviors that would help you alter this pattern. And if you find yourself in chronic conflict with others over your frugal attitudes and actions, performing one of the suggested assignments may prove very useful. You'll stand a better chance of enjoying the benefits of your hoarding without being overly constrained by it.

RONDA, THE WEALTHY
HOARDER

Ronda was a hoarder. She loved to save money. She enjoyed creating a budget and reworking it to make sure she was saving the most that she could. She had a hard time spending money on herself or her husband or on their daughter; in fact, she became highly anxious when she had to spend money on anything at all. Ronda felt compelled to collect coupons, which she stored in boxes under her bed. What was particularly strange about this coupon-saving fetish was that Ronda happened to be exceedingly wealthy. She lived in a magnificent house that had been passed down to her from her parents. Her husband made a substantial living as the head of a thriving business. Eventually, her husband died, and her daughter grew up and moved away. Upon Ronda's death, her daughter came back to pack up and organize her possessions and papers, and found under her mother's bed box after box of alphabetized coupons dating back years! This discovery seemed particularly odd when juxtaposed with another group of items that was also stored in her bedroom: the collection of expensive jewels that Ronda's husband had bought her.

As I mentioned, most hoarders subscribe to the money-equals-security myth. If you have any rigid beliefs in this regard, you may want to go back to chapter 3 from time to time and reread the section on this myth to help you develop a more flexible attitude. This is the best way to work with the mental limitations of excessive hoarding.

Assignments for Hoarders

- Once a week, go out and spend money impulsively on a purchase for your immediate pleasure. Buy an item you would enjoy having that you wouldn't ordinarily allow yourself to buy.

* Once a week, buy a frivolous gift, which you see as a luxury, for someone you care about.

* Once a month, take some portion of money you were going to put into savings or investments (a relatively small amount of money like $25 or $50 is fine) and spend it on yourself or a loved one.

* If you have a budget and you generally consult it often, spend one week or two ignoring your budget and trusting your instincts in deciding what to spend your money on and when. Then compare the results with your budget and see how this experiment went for you.

If you are a spender, you enjoy using your money to buy yourself goods and services for your immediate pleasure. You probably get satisfaction from spending money on gifts for others. The odds are that you have a hard time sav-

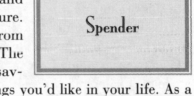

ing money and prioritizing the things you'd like in your life. As a result, it may be difficult for you to put aside enough money for future-oriented purchases and long-term financial goals. You may spend most or all of the money you earn, and you may even be in debt. Now, it is important to realize that some people who are in debt are *not* spenders; they may simply not make enough money to meet their basic needs. If your own income is insufficient to meet your expenses, you are facing a real money crisis. You will have to come up with strategies to generate more income.

One of the common traits of spenders is that they hate making budgets and adhering to them. Some spenders say that having to think about following a budget makes them break out in hives! As a recovering overspender myself, I can attest to the fact that even the word *budget* makes me feel claustrophobic. (Now I know enough to use the term *spending plan* instead.)

If you are an extreme spender, you may feel that you have an addiction or compulsion to spend money. And you may feel ashamed about being out of control in this way. Don't judge yourself too harshly. Remember that you are brainwashed by the media to buy things you don't need and can't afford. Staying sane and balanced in this culture is not easy. So if you are feeling out of control, you are certainly not alone. Even executives at banks have told me that they are great at dealing with other people's money; when it comes to their own money, however, they make unbelievably irrational decisions and act in ways that they do not understand. When you are ready to deal with your chronic overspending, consider joining a free twelve-step program such as Debtors Anonymous. (Appendix B gives you information on how to get in touch with this organization.)

If you are a spender who has enough money to invest, you will tend to value liquidity, although you may need illiquid investments to keep from spending your savings. Spenders usually prefer a high return over safety; they are more interested in having more money around to spend, if they so desire. They are less interested in accumulating money for future security. However, if you are a spender who is dissatisfied with your inability to save, and have difficulty in delaying gratification to meet future goals, you may be ready to recognize the need for investments that will lead to more financial security in the long run. If you are in the process of choosing a financial planner to help you with investment decisions, you will want to find one who is sensitive to your spender tendencies, without being overly critical or judgmental.

CHARLENE, THE SHOPAHOLIC SPENDER

Charlene was a typical spender. She racked up huge credit card bills and always made the minimum payment. Whenever she felt bored or slightly depressed, she would find herself in stores, shopping for clothing for herself and her children—whether she had the money to shop or not. This behavior continued for many years, arousing the wrath of her husband.

When Charlene attended one of my workshops, she realized that she was unconsciously mimicking her mother's spending pattern. A compulsive gambler who periodically ran up a large debit balance, Charlene's mother looked to her husband to bail her out. Her husband, Charlene's dad, would write a check to settle the debt and then ask her to stop this irresponsible behavior. Now contrite, she would promise never to gamble again—till the next time. Charlene, too, would periodically come to her husband in shame and tell him she needed money to pay off her large debt. He'd give her a check and tell her to curb her spending. She'd promise she would and then go out and begin spending again soon after. With the new awareness that she was following a family pattern, Charlene felt ready to take on her addictive spending tendencies once and for all. She joined Debtors Anonymous, came to me for short-term money therapy, and began rewarding herself in more satisfying ways than by spending money she didn't have.

Assignments for Spenders

* Once a week (or once a month), put some amount of money into savings. Decide on the amount that feels right, and stick to that decision.

* Once a week, refrain from making one impulsive purchase.

* Every day for a week, each time you spend money write down how much you're spending and on what. At the end of the week, make a decision about one change you will make (it can be a minor change)

in your spending habits that will lead to less expenditure of money. Decide what you will do with this money you save that will make you feel good about yourself.

DON'T BE SURPRISED AT YOUR OWN EMOTIONAL BACKLASH

Out-of-control spenders often find that when they start to set limits on their spending behavior, they have a big inner tantrum. They feel angry and deprived that they can't buy everything they want whenever the fancy strikes them. If you experience this emotional backlash, don't let it stop you from continuing to practice more responsible ways of handling your money. Your reward will be a boost in your self-esteem and a greater sense of financial security.

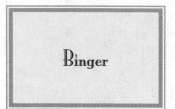

Money bingers are a combination of hoarders and spenders. They tend to save and save, and then blow the money all at once, like a too-tight spring that pops under excessive tension. They often spend large amounts of money on one of their spending binges. During periods of abstinence, bingers may seem quite normal. But they never know when the next binge will hit. If binges become excessive, they can lead to serious overspending and debt. Like excessive spenders, extreme bingers need group support from organizations such as Debtors Anonymous.

HERMAN, THE BINGER

Herman was a typical money binger. He would save money for long periods of time and then go out and buy an expensive car, or a CD player, or a large-screen TV set. Though he earned a good salary as a computer programmer, the problem was that Herman made these huge purchases impulsively and in a trancelike state, whether he had the money for them or not. When he didn't have enough money, he would overcharge on his credit cards or bounce checks for necessities like rent and utilities. His girlfriend felt jerked around by this erratic pattern of spending and saving. She finally persuaded him to take a hard look at the way he made these "decisions" to spend. (Actually, they were more like "attacks" of spending fever. Once they passed, all was calm for a while. But one never knew when the next attack would come.) Herman agreed to begin tracking his spending patterns and his feelings before and after going on a spending spree. He learned an enormous amount about his emotional responses to frustration, longing, deprivation, and stress. And he began to feel in charge of his money for the first time in his life.

COMPULSIVE BARGAIN
HUNTERS

One type of binger is the compulsive bargain hunter. When I was on a TV talk show, the subject was supposed to be "When a Tightwad Marries a Spendthrift," and my role was to help couples resolve these differences. But out came a couple who had a more extreme problem. Paul felt so compelled to buy bargains that he'd gone out and bought a snowmobile even though he and his wife, Yvette, lived in an area where it hardly ever snowed! Why? "Because it was on sale," cracked Yvette. Though the audience had a good laugh, for this couple, chronic overspending was no joke. They had been forced to go to a credit counseling organization for help, and now Paul gave every paycheck to Yvette so she could begin paying off their large debt.

Assignments for Bingers

⌐ Refrain from going on a binge the next time you feel the urge. Instead, write down or notice all your feelings about *not* spending this money. Call a friend to talk about your feelings if possible. Decide what else you could do that would help you feel better about giving up this habitual behavior.

⌐ If refraining from going on binges is too difficult a step, allow yourself to go on a binge but slow down the process. Tape-record, write down, or take stock of your feelings before the binge and afterward. Try to make it a "choreographed" binge, heightening your awareness of the process. Note what you think the binge was supposed to accomplish and whether it did accomplish this.

Money Monk

If you are a money monk, you think that money is dirty, that it is bad, and that if you have too much of it, it will corrupt you. In general, you believe that "money is the root of all evil." It stands to reason that you identify with people of modest means rather than with those who amass wealth. If you happen to come into a windfall somehow (through inheritance, for example), you would tend to be uneasy and even very anxious at the thought of the influx of so much money. You'd worry that you might "sell out," becoming greedier and more selfish, and losing sight of positive human, political, and/or spiritual ideals and values. You would probably avoid investing your money, for fear that it might grow and make you even wealthier. If you were willing to invest some of it, you would most likely be comfortable only with socially responsible investments that reflected your deeper values and convictions and that contributed to causes you would like to support.

SHARON, THE VIRTUOUS MONEY MONK

Sharon was a typical money monk. Educated by the nuns in a Catholic school that instilled the virtues of living simply and rejecting materialism, she went on to become an activist in the 1960s, going on peace marches, volunteering in soup kitchens, and sometimes even organizing demonstrations to oppose the war in Vietnam and end poverty and homelessness in America. When she graduated from college in 1968, she went on to work for a doctor she respected. After several years, he came in and told her he was giving her a large raise. She felt overwhelmed by the amount of the raise and realized in retrospect that her anxiety about having too much money around caused her to begin sabotaging herself at work. Within several months of the raise, she left and began working for a nonprofit organization that paid her a lower salary than the doctor had when she started to work for him. Sharon was back on comfortable and familiar terrain—struggling to pay her bills, having nothing left over for her own personal pleasure and enjoyment.

Years later, in one of my workshops, she gained the insight

that her deep-seated conviction that money would corrupt her had limited her choices and her ability to enjoy life. And even though she never wanted to become a woman who was too wealthy (a "Jackie Onassis," as she described it), she now knew that she could expand her capacity to enjoy her money personally and still express her deeply held convictions about American society and the "right way to live."

Assignments for Money Monks

❧ Spend money on yourself in a way that you have previously considered *selfish* or *decadent*. See if you can experience any enjoyment out of this new behavior.

❧ Spend time imagining yourself coming into a large amount of money and *not* being corrupted by it. How would you feel? What would you do with this money?

❧ Conjure up examples, images, memories of people you've known or read about who have a lot of money and are *not* corrupted by it; people who in fact do many things with their money that you admire and respect. What are your feelings about these people? What do you have in common with them?

Money Avoider

If you tend to be a money avoider, you probably have a hard time balancing your checkbook, paying bills promptly, and doing your taxes until the very last minute. You may avoid making a budget or keeping any kind of financial record. You won't know how much money you have, how much you owe, how much you spend. You may avoid investing money, even if you do have some, because it seems like too much trouble to attend to such details. What fuels this avoidance? You may feel incompetent or overwhelmed when faced with the tasks of your moneylife. If you are an extreme money avoider, you may even feel a kind of money anxiety or paralysis when faced with money tasks that resemble the feelings associated with math anxiety. Some money avoiders share with money monks the belief that money is dirty. Others have a kind of aristocratic disdain toward the boring, seemingly unimportant details of their moneylife. But most avoiders are more prone to feeling that they are inadequate or incompetent in dealing with the complexities and the details of their moneylife, rather than feeling that they are above such dirty work.

Both men and women can be money avoiders. But as we will see in chapter 6, on male-female differences, the moneyphobic woman will act more overtly panicked, anxious, and overwhelmed when faced with money tasks she'd rather avoid, whereas the moneyphobic man will act more calm, cool, and collected while avoiding these tasks. Women will be quicker to admit they feel overwhelmed, in chaos, and ashamed about their avoidance; men's defenses allow them to act as if nothing is amiss at all. But both men and women suffer from an erosion of self-respect if their avoidance continues unabated for too long.

If money avoiders are willing to face these uncomfortable feelings at all, some of them may seek the valuable aid of a financial planner to help them put their finances in order and make some good decisions about how to handle their money. But since money avoiders would probably want planners to take over most of the decision making (so they can keep avoiding it), it is crucial that the avoider find a money professional who is trustworthy and who feels comfortable assuming this much authority and responsibility. Another solution for avoiders is to take on a little more responsibility for their own financial affairs, with a planner's help and guidance.

ELISE, THE MONEY AVOIDER

Elise was a typical avoider. A victim of math anxiety in her early years, she felt a similar money anxiety when she had to balance her checkbook and pay bills. She married a man who became quite wealthy and who always took care of the money. He was quite a bit older than she was, and he always told her not to worry about the money: He'd take care of everything. When he died fairly suddenly, Elise was overwhelmed and in shock. Since she had no experience in dealing with money, she felt panicked about what to do and fearful of making terrible financial decisions and possibly losing all the money her husband had left her. Elise's feelings of incompetence and shame caused her to avoid seeking help for some time, and to avoid making any decisions about her money at all. When she finally visited a financial planner, she had an attack of money anxiety in his office and had trouble filling out the initial information-gathering forms. The planner did one thing for her in that initial session that Elise says she will never forget. He put his hands on her shoulders, looked in her eyes, and told her to relax and trust that she would have all the information and all the help she needed to make good decisions about her money. He also acknowledged her courage in coming to see a planner considering how much anxiety she felt about her financial affairs. With this warm acceptance, Elise did relax, both emotionally and intellectually. Years later, when I met her in a workshop, she confided to me that she had actually learned how to deal with her money quite competently, and that everything had gone very well for her financially as well as emotionally.

Assignments for Money Avoiders

※ Once a week, address one aspect of your moneylife that you usually avoid (e.g., balance your checkbook or set up a system for keeping track of your financial records).

※ If you are procrastinating about a financial task, such as getting information together for taxes, set a time to do it and then *do it*. If you feel enormous resistance to doing this task, invite someone over to be there while you do it, or figure out a way of easing yourself into the task so that it is less unpleasant.

※ If you usually wait a long time to pay bills, deal with them as soon as they arrive.

N.B.: Whether you decide to create your own assignment or to choose one of these and commit to doing it, remember to reward yourself for this new behavior and monitor your feelings about confronting something you usually avoid. Be sure not to reward yourself by allowing yourself to avoid or procrastinate on a different financial task!

If you tend to be a money amasser, you are happiest when you have large amounts of money at your disposal to spend, to save, and/or to invest. If you are not actually spending, saving, or investing, you may feel empty or not fully alive. You tend to equate money with self-worth and power, so a

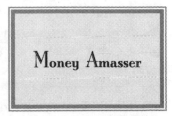

Money Amasser

lack of money may lead to feelings of failure and even depression. If you hire an investment adviser or financial planner, your major concern will be finding investments with high rates of return, since you hope to make as much money as you can as quickly as possible. You probably enjoy making your own financial decisions, so it may be quite difficult for you to give up much control to a money professional. If, on the other hand, you tend to be a worrier, too, and if you are tired of being overly obsessed with your money, you may actually welcome the opportunity to assign some of the details of your moneylife to a trustworthy financial adviser.

KEVIN, THE WORKAHOLIC
MONEY AMASSER

Kevin was a money amasser. He worked long hours to make sure he earned more than enough money. In the evenings and on weekends, he spent hours and hours at the computer, monitoring his investments in the stock market. When he and his wife, Carrie, went on vacations, he saw to it that they stayed in places where he could flaunt how wealthy and successful he was. He bought Carrie expensive furs and jewels, and was proud of how ritzy she looked in them. But even on vacation in Hilton Head, he would spend many hours reading about how to make his money grow. He became increasingly obsessed and more and more boring to his friends and family as the years went by. One day, Carrie finally decided to leave him. Stupefied, he asked, "How can you think about a divorce after all I've given you?" She answered bitterly, "Just the fact that you ask the question that way confirms my feelings that you aren't here with me and haven't been for years. All you think about is your money—how to make it grow, how to flaunt it to impress others. I feel like a showpiece, not like someone you are sharing a life with. I want a real relationship with someone I can talk to." After the shock of his divorce, Kevin began to look at and understand the destructive effect of his obsession with money. In his next relationship, he devoted more time and energy to developing a real connection to his partner. He realized that he couldn't let money run his relationship or his life in general.

Assignments for Money Amassers

❧ Find a time—on a weekend, perhaps, or on vacation—when you can spend at least one day *not* dealing with money at all. You might want to practice this behavior for several weeks in a row, one day a week, and notice if your feelings are evolving in any way over time.

❧ Think about some of your dreams or goals for the future that don't require much money or any money to accomplish, that don't involve making a lot more money, and that might lead to other kinds of pleasure and more solid emotional fulfillment. See if you can move toward taking action on one of these dreams or goals.

❧ Try to remember a moment or period in your life when you were less obsessed with money. What did that feel like? Did you like it? Did you dislike or fear it? Then role-play having this attitude toward money for one day and see how you feel about it now.

If you are a money worrier, you tend to worry about money all the time. You probably want to have a great deal of control over your money. You may spend inordinate amounts of time balancing and rebalancing your check-

Money Worrier

book, checking to see if you have enough money, computing where the money will come from and where it will go. You may spend much of your energy worrying about all the things that could go wrong with your money or about all the terrible things that could happen that would require large amounts of money to fix. Money may well constitute the major preoccupation in your life. You probably believe that if you had a lot more money, you could stop worrying about it. If you are a true money worrier, nothing could be farther from the truth. If you had a lot more money, you would have more money to worry about. (Of course, if your worry comes from a real crisis, such as losing your job or coming down with an unexpected illness, or not having enough money to attend to your basic needs and wants, then it may well be an entirely appropriate response to a temporary stress.)

Many money worriers are also hoarders and amassers. But it is also possible to combine worrying with other money personality types. I would characterize myself, for example, as a recovering spender who has fits of worrying; I also have a smattering of the money monk in me as a throwback to my hippie-activist days. Sounds overwhelming and messy? Actually, it's quite interesting and challenging to work at balancing all these types, and making adjustments in each of them as I progress in my awareness.

GENEVIEVE, THE CHRONIC MONEY WORRIER

Fifty-year-old Genevieve was a chronic money worrier. She worried about money whether she and her husband were doing well in the family business or not. She was forever reworking her budget and always telling her children to watch their money, make sure no one took them for a ride, et cetera, et cetera. When her father died and her mother took ill and came to live with Genevieve and her husband, Genevieve felt so overwhelmed by the expense and the burden of this new responsibility that she went into a deep and paralyzing depression. She was in no condition to find out what sources of support existed for her mother or to take the necessary steps to ensure that her mother was well provided for. When Genevieve came to see me for money therapy, we worked on the chronic aspects of her worrying for several months, and I helped her reach out to her husband, her friends, and to the community around her for support. Slowly, as her chronic worrying decreased, she could take on the real concerns of her difficult situation with her mother and find solutions, both financial and emotional, to help the whole family cope with the stress that comes from caring for an elderly parent in failing health.

Assignments for Worriers

* Give yourself from fifteen minutes to half an hour a day to worry about money actively, in a focused way. Try doing this worrying at the same time every day. Early in the day might be useful, so you are free for the rest of the day to train your consciousness away from money worry. But if you chronically worry in the afternoon, choose that time of day instead. It is best to write down all your worries or speak them into a tape recorder.

* Try assigning every other day to money worry and every other day to abandoning all worry about money. For example, on Monday, Wednesday, and Friday, worry about money as much as you like; reserve Tuesday, Thursday, and Saturday for thinking about, or even worrying about, other things. You decide what to do on Sunday! What's the difference in how you feel during "on" and "off" days?

✹ Once a week for several weeks, consider the following questions: What benefits do you think you get out of worrying about money, and what bad things might happen if you stopped worrying about money? Where do you think these beliefs came from? Where did you learn how to worry about money so much? What would your life be like if there was an absence of worry about money? What scares you about this scenario? What would you like about it?

Risk takers and risk avoiders (see the following section) are the two remaining money types. Both are concerned strictly with investing styles. If you are in a couple relationship, it's quite common for one member of a couple to be a risk taker and the other a risk avoider, and for these opposing tendencies to be a source of friction in the relationship. If you are in a relationship, do you and your partner fit this pattern?

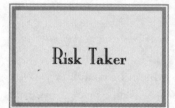

If you are the risk taker, you enjoy taking risks with your money. You like the thrill and the adventure of taking a risk and riding the waves to what you hope will be a positive outcome. To you, safety and security, and any excessive planning in connection with your money, are like a straitjacket that limits your behavior and your financial options. You tend to invest lump sums into one investment with hopes of "hitting the jackpot." For many risk takers, the thrill and intensity of the ride is more important than reaching the destination. But some will become extremely distressed and depressed when their risk-taking behavior ends in financial loss. Risk takers tend to focus on the old adage that "the greatest risks bring the greatest rewards," ignoring the possibility that they may also bring the greatest losses.

Assignments for Risk Takers

❧ Once a week, practice planning out purchases, investments, or savings in a more conservative mode than usual.

❧ Take some money out of a high-risk investment and put it into a conservative low-risk one.

❧ Spend one whole week refraining from taking *any* financial risks. See if you can look for pleasure in other areas of your life.

❧ Think about, and describe in detail, if possible, any memories or models from your childhood that may have had a hand in your growing up to be a risk taker.

N.B.: When you perform one of these assignments or an exercise of your own choosing, you can expect to feel bored, frustrated, trapped—even depressed. Take my word for it that these feelings will pass and that eventually you will experience some benefits from operating in a more conservative mode.

If you tend to be a risk avoider, you choose safety and security in your financial affairs above all else. You probably like to budget to avoid "surprises." When you invest, you are happiest with low-risk investments that  yield low rewards. You tend not to care about liquidity; you prefer investments that will give you and your family security in the future, especially during your retirement years. To you, planning feels like contentment and security. Taking a financial risk feels like jumping off a cliff because you are certain it will end in catastrophe. You have a hard time imagining how anyone could enjoy that experience. You surely couldn't!

As with the other money types, if being a risk avoider is not a problem for you, you need not read any farther.

Assignments for Risk Avoiders

♦ Once a week, take some financial action that seems risky to you: it might be a spontaneous purchase or a choice of a slightly risky new investment.

♦ Imagine, in as much detail as possible, taking a financial risk and having it pan out very well. Imagine all the feelings you would have about taking the risk and about the positive outcome. If one of your distant fantasies does involve more financial risk than you are usually comfortable with, imagine what you could do to move closer to taking this risk, perhaps in a more limited way.

♦ Take some money (it can be a small amount, such as $25 or $50) out of savings or out of a safe investment, and put it into a riskier investment that might yield high returns. What are your feelings as you invest the money and as you wait for the financial outcome?

♦ Think about, and describe in detail if possible, why you believe you've taken this stance of risk avoidance. (Maybe you've been influenced by a traumatic event or by the example of someone who took a high risk only to be wiped out financially.)

N.B.: It can be *very* difficult to start taking risks with your money. You must accept it on faith that your anxious feelings will give way in time to a new sense of self-confidence and creativity as you expand your risk tolerance.

Now that we have completed our examination of the basic money types, I want to stress the point that each type exhibits some positive attributes as well as some limitations and tendencies toward imbalance. Hoarders are good at budgeting, prioritizing, and delaying gratification.

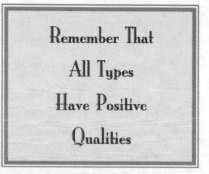

Remember That All Types Have Positive Qualities

Spenders are generous with themselves and others, and know how to enjoy life in the moment. Money monks have a high degree of moral integrity and are committed to noble ideals. Money amassers understand the benefits of money in many different ways. Worriers usually keep track of their money well and are responsible about money. Avoiders don't let money take up too much space in their lives and are often quite involved in other areas of their life in a constructive way. Risk takers know the value of risk, and risk avoiders know the value of safety.

Whatever combination of money types you tend to be, you'll profit from identifying all the attitudes and behaviors that you would like to change and the best ways of making these changes.

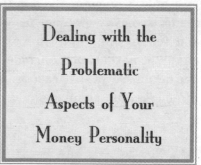

Dealing with the Problematic Aspects of Your Money Personality

 * Which money personality traits are controlling you or are out of balance in some way?

❧ Which traits create tension in your relationships?

❧ Which traits seem to be the most rigid or chronic?

❧ In general, do you want to change your behavior, your underlying attitudes, or both?

❧ Which of these negative traits are you willing to confront directly, by practicing the nonhabitual over a period of time?

❧ What kinds of assignments work best for you in doing what doesn't come naturally?

❧ What kinds of rewards provide the most positive reinforcement without encouraging the old dysfunctional behaviors?

❧ What is the best way for you to monitor your reactions to new behaviors, and to track your progress? Does it work best to write down your reactions, to record them, or to close your eyes and visualize how you feel when you practice these new actions or try on new attitudes? Would drawing pictures about your reactions be useful to you?

As you notice more and more about your money personality over time, you can make adjustments, some subtle and some dramatic, so that your money personality is a blend of styles that suits you well, free of rigidity and extreme imbalances or compulsions.

In the next chapter, on money dialogues, you will learn to practice the most evocative exercise I know of for getting at—and transforming—your core issues and conflicts in connection with money.

5

Money Dialogues: Tools for

Growth and Transformation

When I first began teaching men and women about money harmony more than ten years ago, I feared that people might react negatively to my idea that we all have a relationship with money that is analogous to a relationship with a person; and that if we use this metaphor to explore our relationship with money (e.g., its current status, the major past influences, the changes that need to be made), we can discover an amazing array of irrationalities that block us from using our money wisely.

In the same vein, when I took an old gestalt therapy exercise and fashioned it into an assignment I called a "money dialogue," I feared that most people would find it too weird and kinky to do this work, that no one except a few uninhibited individuals would be able to create a money dialogue with the proper degree of spontaneity or abandon. Happily, I was wrong.

Most people have been willing to create money dialogues—and have gleaned a tremendous amount of information from them.

Some have even found the assignment fun to do! And now, after years of reading and hearing hundreds of these dialogues, I must say, to adapt a famous quote by Will Rogers, "I never met a money dialogue I didn't like." They are always revealing and often funny, touching, or profound.

I invite you to consider creating one or more money dialogues of your own. You might even enjoy preparing money dialogues as much as I've enjoyed reading and hearing them through the years.

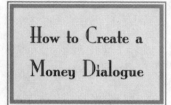

Let's start by imagining that Money is a person with whom you are having a relationship. Imagine having a conversation with Money about how your relationship is going. If this seems hard for you to do, try imagining that Money is being interviewed on a TV talk show. What would Money say about how you are treating him/her/it? For example, if you are a spender, Money might say, "He throws me around; he doesn't treat me with respect." If you are a hoarder, Money might complain, "She holds on to me so tight, I'm choking to death!" If you are a money monk, Money might remark, "He thinks I'm dirty; what a self-righteous guy!" When you conjure up this funny picture of Money being interviewed on a talk show, it becomes easier for you to visualize Money as a person with whom you are actually having a relationship.

Now let's create a dialogue with Money by talking to it (him/her) directly. (I suggest that you either write down your money dialogue or speak it into a tape recorder.) Here are five steps to follow for preparing not only the dialogue but also an "internal commentary" on it:

1. Have a conversation with Money about how the relationship is going.* The length of the conversation varies according to the individual. Just let it continue for as long as it takes for you to feel it winding down of its own accord. Go at your own pace, and try to record this conversation as spontaneously as you can. Let yourself be surprised with what emerges. If any picture of what Money looks like comes into your head, you might even want to draw a picture or describe any details or images of how Money looks to you.

2. Have your mother (the voice of your mother in your head, that is) comment on the dialogue you've just written, as if she has just finished reading it. This commentary should be quite brief—a sentence or two, or a short paragraph at most.

3. Have your father comment on the dialogue. Sometimes, fathers (or mothers) have no comment at all and respond with silence. Of course, that's significant too. But if you can imagine what Dad would be thinking after reading your money dialogue, have him say it.

4. Have any other powerful influences from the past comment on your money dialogue. For example, if you are divorced, your ex-spouse might have something to say. Or your grandmother or grandfather, a godparent, a religious teacher, your best friend—anyone who influenced your relationship with money.

5. Have God, or your Higher Power, or your inner voice of wisdom, comment on the dialogue you've just written.

In the following sections, you'll be reading a number of sample money dialogues that will give you a greater understanding of five

---

* If you are having trouble creating this conversation and are feeling stuck, you can turn to the sample money dialogues in this chapter. But if possible, I recommend doing your own dialogue first and reading the sample dialogues later.

money types (spender, hoarder, avoider, money monk, and money amasser).

Olivia's Money Dialogue: A Spender's World

As a recovering overspender myself, I'll share with you the first money dialogue I wrote:

MONEY: You never seem to be able to hold on to me long enough to satisfy your important long-range goals. What's your problem?

OLIVIA: I feel alive and happy only when I'm spending you. When I'm not spending you, I feel deprived, empty, depressed.

MONEY: That's seeing only one side of what I can do for you. You're like a spoiled kid who can't wait for anything she wants.

OLIVIA: It's true; I know how to indulge myself in my whims, but not how to treat myself well in the deepest sense. So instead of attacking me, how about helping me with this?

MONEY: It's not in my power to do that. I'm just a bunch of dollars and cents. Maybe your husband, friends, or a therapist could help you with how you deal with me. Frankly, I'm at a loss.

OLIVIA: Maybe if I could focus on my long-term money needs, I could save you more for future security, investments, et cetera. And maybe I could explore new ways to nurture myself, instead of running out and buying clothing when I feel depressed.

MONEY: Sounds good to me. Just please try to throw me around less and show me a little respect.

OLIVIA: I'll try.

OLIVIA'S INTERNAL
COMMENTARY

MOM: Why not indulge yourself as I did? Life is short, and it's too
bad you and I didn't find men who could give us all that we
really wanted. On the other hand, you are kind of a spoiled brat
and need to learn some self-control!

DAD: I think you're doing okay, dear, but I worry about your future
security. Like Mom, I'm sorry you didn't find a rich husband to
take care of all this for you.

GOD: Sorry your parents don't have the advice you need to hear.
But you're on the right track. Following some of your husband's
good advice about money makes sense. And pursuing your
deeper, real needs is definitely the way to stop your self-indul-
gent and compulsive spending. The more you love yourself and
increase your self-esteem, the more money will assume its proper
role in proper perspective. You are on the right track.

Notice that I did not include comments from anyone other than
Mom, Dad, and God. That's because their powerful voices were the
only ones I heard.

Fred is a hoarder whose father was
raised in dire poverty in a large working-class family, and who emulated his
father's fear and tightness about
money. His wife, Marie, criticizes him
constantly for his extreme hoarding
tendencies.

Fred's Money
Dialogue:
A Hoarder's
World

MONEY: You never take me anywhere.
You hold on to me so tight, I'm getting squeezed to death!

FRED: I'm so afraid if I spend you, you'll disappear altogether. My dad told me we could lose everything unless we were extremely careful with every penny, and I believed him.

MONEY: How long are you gonna keep living as if you're in dire straits? You make good money now, and you don't enjoy it at all.

FRED: But what about security for the future? Don't I have to start saving now for my old age?

MONEY: Yes, but not as extremely and compulsively as you do. . . . Why, look at the stress it causes in your marriage, and notice how guilty and stingy you feel inside for being so tight that they call you "Squeak"!

FRED: It's true, I don't like it much. But I'm afraid that if I change and loosen up at all, I'll lose everything.

MONEY: Oh brother! Are you a tough case!

FRED'S INTERNAL
COMMENTARY

DAD: You're right, son! You can never have too much money in the bank or too much security for the future. Don't let money seduce you into foolishness. You never know when the ground might get shaky under your feet. You have to be prepared for the worst.

MOM: Well, dear, as long as you're making a good living, I don't see why you have to worry that much . . . though your dad *is* usually right about these things. Even though we never had many frills, we didn't starve, either. I'm grateful that your dad was such a hard worker, and that he was never frivolous with our money. We went without meals sometimes so that we could manage to send you kids to college and grad school, and I'm proud that we were able to do all that.

MARIE: I can't stand listening to you talk about money. Your constant hoarding and worrying make me want to scream! As long as you keep being so tight, I'll keep squirreling money away on the sly and spending out of angry rebellion.

HIGHER POWER: It's time to experiment with giving in to more spontaneity and pleasure. You can trust yourself that if you do, you won't go overboard and become a crazy overspender. You *are* wise enough to find true balance if you begin practicing trust and relaxation now.

Myrna is a money avoider. So intense is her money anxiety that she puts off all dealings with her moneylife till the last possible moment. Her extreme form of avoidance exasperated her ex-husband, Paul, and contributed to the breakup of her marriage.

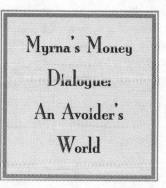

Myrna's Money Dialogue: An Avoider's World

MONEY: Why do you always avoid dealing with me? You treat me like a leper!

MYRNA: You make me feel incompetent and overwhelmed. I'd prefer it if I *never* had to deal with you!

MONEY: I'm *not* the one who makes you feel this way. But the more you avoid me, the more of a pain in the neck I become. I can't go away altogether. You need me to function.

MYRNA: I know, and I resent that terribly. I just wish someone else in my life would take care of you for me.

MONEY: Sorry, but there's no one around who will. What makes dealing with me so awful? I'm not a monster, you know—just dollars and cents.

MYRNA: No one ever taught me about how to treat you, how to take care of you. I don't know how to begin.

MONEY: One step at a time, of course. There are others around who could help you, you know. They just can't rescue you. Once you start paying some more attention to me, you'll see, I'm not such a bad guy after all. I just don't like to be ignored.

MYRNA'S INTERNAL
COMMENTARY

MOM: I always told you that you were incompetent around money. Just like your dad. I hope you hire someone else to handle your money for you. You'll *never* be able to do it yourself!

DAD: I never had a head for figures. Other things were more important to me. People were my strong suit. Luckily, your mom took care of the whole thing for me. She was good at managing money. But she made me fell like a worm for not being able to do it myself.

PAUL: Grow up and begin taking responsibility for yourself. Otherwise, no man will put up with your extreme helplessness—I sure couldn't!

GOD: Forgive yourself for your fears and avoidance. I've already forgiven you. If you start taking small steps to take on money tasks you usually avoid, while tolerating your uncomfortable feelings about money, you will get the job done. The sooner you start, the quicker your self-esteem will rise. Once you start exercising your own muscles, you will have all the help you need to get the job done. Money will then feel like a friend, rather than a source of anxiety and fear.

Ricky is a typical money monk. Not only was he brought up in a religious school where he was taught that money was evil, but in the 1960s he became an activist who vowed he would never be identified with "those corrupt wealthy schmucks in the military-industrial complex." His dialogue elucidates his mind-set clearly.

> Ricky's Money Dialogue: A Money Monk's World

MONEY: You act like I'm the devil or something. The way you back away from me in horror makes no sense!

RICKY: I gotta make sure I don't have too much of you around, or I risk selling out, becoming bourgeois, fat, and lazy—if not downright greedy and corrupt.

MONEY: I don't have the power to corrupt you. Some people have a lot of me and treat me well. We have a good time together, and we don't do anyone any harm.

RICKY: Yeah? Name two people you know who are like that. All the people I respect are struggling financially just as I am. They know the value of a dollar, and they know it's better not to get too comfortable and smug.

MONEY: Boy, I hope you open your eyes before it's too late. Otherwise, your spartan existence might catch up with you, and our war will just escalate over time—from your end, I mean. Grow up, kiddo; you don't have to suffer to be virtuous.

RICKY: Mmmm . . . I'll think about that . . . though I still don't trust you. Maybe all this is just a con.

RICKY'S INTERNAL
COMMENTARY

MOM: Honey, you really don't have to deny yourself so many com-
forts. Now that I'm getting older, I wish your life were a little
easier materially and in other ways.

DAD: Son, I'm proud that you've stayed such a simple person in the
midst of this world of corruption. Don't give in; keep resisting
temptation in the form of money.

FATHER LUKE: Waste not, want not, my son. Don't give in to the
seduction of money and things. Live simply, and live by your
true spiritual values of simplicity and self-sacrifice.

GOD: There is no need to starve yourself so that others may eat.
Look for examples all around you of those who have money and
use it well. It might be more creative and enlightening for you to
experience having money and using it well to reflect your deepest
values than to make sure you don't have it around.

Arlene's Money Dialogue: An Amasser's World

Arlene is a money amasser who was brought up in a poor family. Her parents separated when she was young, and her mother struggled to support her and her three siblings. Her mother's bitterness at her father's failure to make a good living and to pay child support was communicated to her daughter throughout her childhood. Arlene vowed never to be as poor and struggling as her overworked mother. In her growing-up years, she was very close to her aunt Irene, who owned a dress shop and worked constantly to make more and more money, until she married a wealthy lawyer when she was in her forties.

MONEY: Boy, you pay me so much attention, sometimes I just wish you'd give me a rest!

ARLENE: I can never get enough of you to relax and feel satisfied. The more of you I have around at all times, the happier and safer I feel.

MONEY: Yeah, but I'm getting exhausted from being constantly spent, saved, invested, reinvested, flaunted, and on and on. I mean, I like *some* attention, but this is ridiculous.

ARLENE: With you around, I feel I'm worth something . . . that others will respect me and not put me down. Maybe I can even use you to find a rich husband so I'll have more of you around. I wouldn't mind working less and still enjoying you more and more.

MONEY: Not only are you obsessed, but you want something for nothing. It's a dangerous trip, my girl!

ARLENE: Well, I'm not ready to give it up—not until I have at least a million of you around. Then I'll *think* about it. And you work for me, not the other way around. Remember that, buddy!

MONEY: Some buddy!

ARLENE'S INTERNAL
COMMENTARY

MOTHER: Stick to your guns, kid. I wish I were as good as you are at getting money in large quantities. Then I wouldn't have had to struggle and feel like a nobody.

DAD: Your mother and you are both crass materialists of the worst kind. I'm glad I got away from the two of you. Money isn't everything, you know. I had a much happier life than your mom, and I still don't have a lot of money.

AUNT IRENE: I hope you end up wealthier than all the men in your life. If you have enough money, you don't need people much. Of course, if you are lucky enough to find a rich husband as I did, so much the better!

INNER VOICE: It's time to look at what's driving you so hard about getting more and more money. It will never make up for your years of deprivation and struggle with your mother, or for the lack of fathering in your childhood. If you get money down to its proper role in your life, you will be able to relax and enjoy your life—now. Otherwise, you will feel you never have enough of it, and you will continue to be driven by, and to sacrifice relationships to, this pursuit of money. Love yourself a little more, and worship money a little less.

What You Can Learn from Your Own Money Dialogue

What will this dialogue tell you? First, it will give you a more in-depth picture of how your life with money is really going, what are the sticking points or conflicts involved, what are the strengths and weaknesses. Second, it will give you a better handle on the influences from your past. And finally, through the voice of God (or Higher Power, or inner wisdom), it will help you see what direction you need to move in and some step you can take or some attitude you can adopt to evolve toward more harmony in your moneylife.

Sometimes Money itself functions as a kind of inner wisdom or Higher Power in the dialogue. That's fine, too. There are no wrong ways to do a money dialogue. Whatever you come up with can be used to heighten your awareness about yourself, your money, and what money harmony would look like for you.

What strikes you most strongly about your own money dialogue? What have you learned, or been reminded of, or what has affected you emotionally? What insights has it given you that may help you in your search for balance in your moneylife?

Money dialogues can be done again and again. Each time your dialogue will evolve a little, as your relationship with money becomes clearer and more conscious. If you tune in to your own sense of timing, you'll know whether to do these dialogues once a month, every other week, once a week, or every day for a week. In any case, creating money dialogues periodically will help you track your movement toward money harmony and, little by little, remove the blocks along the way.

The money dialogue is a powerful assignment. Do not underestimate its power to shake loose old dysfunctional attitudes and behaviors and to move you toward balance in your moneylife. By paying attention to, and following through on, the insights gleaned from your dialogue, you are taking responsibility for turning your relationship with money into one that fulfills your real needs.

With the creation of your own money dialogue, you have completed the first half of your journey toward money harmony. Now you are ready to begin looking at differences between men and women in the area of money.

PART TWO

❧

The

Couples Component

of Money Harmony

6.

Male-Female Differences Around Money: Understanding Two Different Cultures

In the spring of 1983, my husband and I went with four other couples to see a one-man comedy show called "Defending the Caveman," in which Rob Becker presented a brilliant, hilarious analysis of many of the differences between men and women. The premise of his routine was that most of these differences stemmed from the fact that men were trained, in caveman times, to be hunters, whereas women learned to be gatherers. Male hunters focused on one point and one point only—the rear of the animal to be killed—and performed this primary survival task in silence. A man gained status in the community by killing more animals than the other men did. Women gatherers, on the other hand, chitchatted with their female friends as they went to the fields to gather berries, medicinal herbs, et cetera, in cooperative harmony. Becker dramatized a myriad of ways in which these differences are manifested today and cause problems for both men and women in their couple relationships. Take shopping, for instance: men go to a store and "kill the shirt" they need, wear it till it wears out or "dies," and then go "kill" another one(!); women "gather" clothes they might eventually like to wear. To illustrate how men tend to compete whereas women tend to cooperate, Becker acted out different scenarios when groups of men or women are standing around an empty potato chip bowl at a party. Women go as a group to replace the chips, chatting all the while and never missing a beat; men negotiate among themselves about who will have to go do it, with each man trying to avoid the task if possible. Becker also reminded us that men hate to ask for directions when lost, whereas women are willing and even eager to seek help.

My friends and I laughed till our sides hurt and eyed each other slyly, recognizing ourselves and our mates again and again. Behind our laughter was a deep and healing recognition that many of our conflicts stemmed from being trained to perform different roles in life, and having a worldview that reflected those divergent roles.

In this chapter, we will be focusing on male-female differences around money. I suggest that you think of men and women as coming from two completely different cultures, so that you can cultivate an attitude of both detachment and curiosity. It will also help if, like Rob Becker, you can see the humor in the differences between the sexes.

It is dangerous to generalize about men and women in any area, and looking at your moneylife in this way poses similar risks. For every generalization, there are a great number of exceptions, and those of you who don't fit the stereotypes may feel alienated or demeaned by these descriptions.* But since many of these differences do seem gender-based, for the simplicity of this discussion, I will talk about differences between women and men.

---

* Gay couples who have come to me for therapy have taught me through the years that with certain behaviors, it is better to talk about who holds the masculine role and who embodies the feminine role, rather than talking about male and female per se. But there are other areas in which these male-female differences seem to apply, even to gay couples.

As a practicing psychotherapist for more than twenty years, I have always been particularly fascinated by couples conflicts and male-female differences. My observations stem from my own work with couples and my reflections on my own couple relationship, as well as those of my friends and colleagues. I am not a research psychologist or an expert in statistical trends, and thus the following discussion must be understood as my own professional and personal observations, and not as "absolute truth." This said, however, I do believe that if you reflect with me on the wide range of differences between many men and women, which run the gamut from perceptions and experiences to communication and investment styles, you will be better able to empathize with your partner and create a positive and respectful climate for moneytalks and mutual goal setting.*

The differences in the socialization patterns of men and women are manifested in a number of areas. These differences have a profound effect on their behaviors and attitudes around money.

Socialization

Patterns

SENSE OF BOUNDARIES

In most cases, the mother is the primary caregiver in the family. To become a normal adult, a child must separate from his or her

* Victoria Felton-Collins, in her excellent book *Couples and Money: Why Money Interferes with Love and What to Do About It*, written with Suzanne Blair Brown (New York: Bantam rack edition, 1992), explores male-female differences about money more comprehensively than anyone in the field. Her perspective mirrors my own very closely, and in this chapter I draw on some of her material: see chapter 2, "Men, Women, and the Money Game They Play," pp. 29–50, and chapter 3, "Power Plays, Paybacks, and Other Bad Investments," pp. 51–70.

mother and develop a sense of personal boundaries. Since men need to make a clear distinction between themselves and their parent of the opposite sex, they tend to develop more solid, and sometimes even rigid, personal boundaries. They tend to hold on to their separate sense of self, even when in a relationship. Women, on the other hand, have a more fluid, and sometimes more merged, sense of being in a relationship. Separating from their parent of the same sex does not have to be such a distinct and clear process of boundary definition. Thus, women tend to be more comfortable with merging and connectedness in relationships. It will be helpful to keep these boundary differences in mind when we look at common gender-based differences in styles of financial decision making, patterns of healing from angers and hurts, and preferences for joint or separate money.

COMPETITION AND COOPERATION

In general, women were raised to be accommodators, to avoid conflict, to be "nice," giving, and tuned in to other people's needs—in short, to live in a world of cooperation; men, on the other hand, were raised to value competition, to cultivate qualities of assertiveness and aggressiveness to get ahead and to win power and position, and tend to experience the world more from a perspective of hierarchy.* A fair number of men are also trained to function cooperatively in some environments, such as in team sports or in the workplace (where they serve as corporate "team players"). But in many settings, even if they are capable of cooperative attitudes

---

* In *You Just Don't Understand: Women and Men in Conversation* (New York: Ballantine, 1990), Deborah Tannen discusses these and many related differences between the sexes in chapter 6, "Community and Context: Styles in Conflict," pp. 149–87.

and behaviors, most men tend to internalize the world from the perspective of hierarchy and competition. In intimate relationships at home, it is easy for a man to feel either one-up or one-down rather than on the same level as his mate. When men and women come together, these differences are manifested with regard to who controls the money; who makes the major financial decisions in the family, how men and women give to charity, and how they talk about money, both alone and together.

DEFENSES AROUND FEELING
NEEDY OR VULNERABLE

Because women were raised in an atmosphere of accommodation and cooperation, many women are comfortable expressing their feelings and even their vulnerability about their own failings or sense of self. A number of women grow up to feel that being dependent on men is in some contexts okay, or even endearing. Raised to compete and win, men tend to think that expressing weaknesses, acting or feeling needy, and acting or being dependent in any way are "unmasculine," "wimpy," and thus unacceptable attitudes and behaviors. These divergent emotional styles will of course come into play when men and women try to have moneytalks, when they grapple with situations in which the woman makes more money than the man, and when they try to look at various other aspects of their moneylife together.

"THINKING" AND
"FEELING" TYPES

Researchers who have been working with the Myers-Briggs Type Personality Indicator have adopted Carl Jung's terminology when describing the way people tend to make decisions and resolve issues in their lives. They identify "thinking" types as those who tend to be more objective, detached, logical, and analytical. "Feeling" types are more subjective, humane, and concerned with harmony when making decisions and discussing issues.* Where thinkers value firmness and clarity and want to be just and fair, feeling types tend to value persuasion, harmony of the group or unit, and are concerned with social values as opposed to setting policy. Myers-Briggs researchers have found that approximately six out of ten men are thinking types, and six out of ten women are feeling types.† Bill Jeffries, a highly respected trainer and author in the Myers-Briggs field, tells me that practitioners find that in over 90 percent of marriages, men and women choose mates of the opposite type right from the start. Furthermore, I have found in my own work with couples that they will polarize into oppositional modes about just about everything (see chapter 7 for details), and the difference between thinking and feeling types is no exception. So even in the somewhat rare cases where both members of a couple are thinkers, the more extreme thinking type exhibits this tendency to an even greater extent, and his or her mate will act more like a feeling type by comparison. Among the couples I've worked with through the years, it is most often the man who acts more imper-sonal and detached, and the woman is the one who takes care of everyone's feelings, shares more emotional, subjective reactions, and works toward the harmony of the couples unit. Understanding these opposing tendencies will be useful in later sections, when the

---

* This comparison of decision-making styles is found in *Type Talk: The 16 Personality Types That Determine How We Live, Love, and Work*, by Otto Kroeger and Janet M. Thuesen (New York: Dell, 1988), p. 28.

† David Keirsey and Marilyn Bates, *Please Understand Me: Character and Temperament Types* (Del Mar, Calif.: Prometheus Nemesis, 1984), p. 20. This statistic is found in many books by Myers-Briggs practitioners. A number of authors say that the statistic is closer to two-thirds; that is, two-thirds of men are thinking types, and two-thirds of women are feeling types.

discussion turns to the selection of financial advisers and the conducting of moneytalks.

Bear in mind that I am *not* implying that feeling types are incapable of logical, rational discussion and decision making, or that thinking types do not have strong feelings. I am merely describing ways in which these types tend to make decisions and move toward action.

TRAINING AROUND COMPETENCE AND SELF-CONFIDENCE

In spite of societal changes over the last twenty years, I think it is still fair to say that many women were raised with the belief, whether overt or unconscious, that dealing with finances was men's job. Many of us were told, either directly or in subtler ways, that if we were lucky, we would find some rich man to take care of us and to deal with the unpleasant tasks of money management. We were raised to be nurturers of these men first, and competent achievers second or not at all. No one expected us to know how to manage money competently, and certainly, no one took the time to teach us about it. Furthermore, gender-biased educational systems have often led us to undermine and doubt our own areas of genuine knowledge and understanding. Thanks to growing awareness of gender-biased societal messages and attempts to correct these imbalances, we are seeing many younger women who, happily, were raised to believe that they could become and accomplish almost anything they set their mind on. Thus, I have encountered in recent years more women in their late teens, twenties, and early thirties who have a more solid sense of self-empowerment and competence. But despite this new progress, I still find that many women have vestiges of fear that they won't be able to be competent enough about managing and making money to truly take care of themselves in the best way they can. And even among younger women, I hear echoes of the time-honored dream, "If only some wealthy and successful man would come and take care of all this for me . . ." I believe that the old social traditions die very slowly—more slowly than many of us women would like to acknowledge.

Men, on the other hand, are generally expected to know how to handle their money; they are treated as if they do understand the ins and outs of money, whether they were overtly taught about it or not. One problem that many men have confronted is the expectation that, like sex, money was something they should just know about, without ever having been specifically instructed in the wise use of their money. Many men are trained to mask their areas of incompetence, and they assume an air of authority whether it is justified or not. If vulnerability is not okay for men, incompetence is even more of an anathema. When we talk about differences in defenses, we will see how these attitudes can create tension in male-female communication about money and in the assigning of responsibility and blame.

Financial Power in Adulthood

You may remember the old nursery rhyme, "Clap hands, clap hands till Daddy gets home. Daddy has money, and Mommy has none!" The words of this rhyme still ring true for many of us. In 1980, 88 percent of American men were earning more money than their wives; in 1990, 80 percent made more than their wives.* In many cases, men are

---

* Donald Katz quotes these statistics in a magazine article entitled "Men, Women, and Money: The Last Taboo," in *Worth*, June 1993, p. 58.

paid more than women for the same or similar jobs. Not only do men make more money than women, but they wield more authority and power in top-level positions in big business and government. The heads of major corporations are almost exclusively men. Women, for their part, find that they come up against the "glass ceiling."

These differences in ability to earn money and in experience with assuming power and authority lead to vast disparities in feelings of competence and self-confidence, both in the outside world and at home. They affect the ways in which men and women talk about money with each other and make decisions about money, both alone and together. Finally, these differences have an enormous impact on couple relationships: partners do not wield power over money to the same degree, nor do they have the same financial burdens and fears.

From everything that's been said in the preceding sections, it stands to reason that men and women have different ways of showing confidence and insecurity around money. These differences are clearly manifested when they consult with financial planners. According to my friends in this field, female clients who feel insecure about their financial

Defenses Around Confidence, Self-confidence, and Money

knowledge tend to act more overtly "moneyphobic"; some even experience a kind of panicky, paralyzing anxiety around money. Planners should try to help these women through their panic so they can recognize their real strengths and start looking at their money in a more objective fashion. Male clients, on the other hand, tend to act confident and knowledgeable about money—even when they aren't. So when planners find that they need to explain things to men, they typically say something like, "I realize that you know this already, but I'll run it by you anyway just to make sure you haven't missed anything."

If these defenses are in place when women and men come together in a couple relationship to talk about money, the woman will be more overtly emotional and anxious, and the man will act competent and in control, even if he isn't. Only if both members are willing to work with their defenses can they remove these chronic "masks" and deal with the issues at hand.

ASSIGNING BLAME AND TAKING CREDIT

With these different defenses about money, men and women react to their own financial successes and failures in completely opposite ways. When men make money in the stock market, for example, they tend to take the credit, attributing the successful outcome to their own cleverness and financial acumen. Where they lose money on their investments, they tend to put the blame on their advisers. When women make money in the stock market, they credit outside influences, such as their advisers, or sheer good fortune. When they lose money, they tend to blame themselves. Since men are raised to be competitive "winners" and to hide their vulnerability, it is easy to see why they project their blame on others. And since women are raised to be accommodators, and to accept a stance of vulnerability and dependency, it is understandable that their first impulse is to swallow blame and to deflect credit.

A female friend of mine in her forties told me a story that illustrates the kind of burden that many men carry with regard to work and money. A wealthy doctor who was a friend of her parents once drove her to his house for Thanksgiving dinner. She had always envied

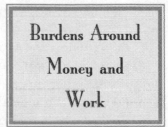

Burdens Around Money and Work

this successful man, thinking that with all his wealth and possessions, he must be very happy and content with his life. But during that trip in the car, he surprised her by unburdening himself. "You have no idea," he said, "how draining it is to work fifteen hours a day so that my wife and kids can live a life of leisure in the suburbs." My friend was startled by the bitterness and sadness in his voice, which jarred her into a realization that perhaps this man's life was not as enjoyable as she had imagined, and certainly had its share of stress and unfulfillment despite his material wealth.

Despite all the economic and social changes over the past few decades, many men, if not most of them, still feel that the responsibility to be the main breadwinner in the family is on their shoulders. Men tend to envy women for having certain options in the workplace that they feel they cannot exercise themselves: to work part-time (or maybe not at all), or to pursue the job or career that brings the greatest personal satisfaction rather than the biggest paycheck. Until our system is truly more egalitarian, men need our sympathy, and our appreciation, for carrying such a heavy burden of work in so many cases. A great number of men also feel burdened because they have taken the primary responsibility for managing and investing the money in the family. They long for women to share this burden with them and to be able to talk with them about the nitty-gritty financial details. Finally, many men complain that though they make more money than women, it is the women who are spending it. Warren Farrell cites statistics to indicate this may well be true. He notes that both men and women tend to use discretionary income to buy gifts for women, and that many men feel that they work long and hard without ever reaping the fruits of their labors in economic terms.*

Women, on the other hand, feel the burden of the "second shift." In most families, they still are the primary caregivers of their children, and the ones who take most of the responsibility for keeping their homes clean. Yet they are likely to hold down a full-time job outside the home as well. Thus, many exhausted women find themselves trying to be superwomen who juggle all their tasks and roles without complaining or feeling overwhelmed. When women show resistance to learning and practicing money management and investment skills, part of the reason may be that they don't feel they can take on yet another job. Women need our empathy and appreciation for the complex burdens they carry in diverse areas of their lives.

In households where men make more money than women—and, as I've noted, this is still the case in 80 percent of marriages—many women resent their economic dependency on men and the feeling of lack of control that this engenders. Indeed, after divorce, women's economic status declines as much as 50 percent (whereas men's suicide rate doubles, a statistic that reflects their difficulty in soliciting help when in crisis, and in expressing and resolving emotional trauma).†

---

* In *The Myth of Male Power* (New York: Simon and Schuster, 1993), Warren Farrell explores men's sense of burden and powerlessness, and gives dramatic examples and statistics to indicate that the situation in which many men find themselves in our culture is no more enviable than that of many women.

† These statistics are cited in Aaron R. Kipnis and Elizabeth Hingston's article "Ending the Battle Between the Sexes," *UTNE Reader*, January/February 1993, pp. 69–76 (a special issue entitled *Men and Women: Can We Get Along? Should We Even Try?*). They argue that men and women should first split off into same-sex groups where they can talk and empathize with others who have similar burdens and then meet and communicate together to better understand each other's separate burdens.

When couples try to have moneytalks together, instead of arguing over which partner is carrying the more onerous burden, they need to take the time and develop the empathy necessary to acknowledge the real and separate burdens they each carry in trying to make their joint lives work both economically and emotionally.

Because of women's history of chronic economic dependency, first on their parents and then on their mates, they tend to have global, cataclysmic fears about losing all their money and ending up on the street. Even wealthy women with large inheritances have reported 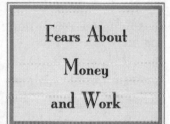 that they share this "bag lady nightmare." I believe that the roots of this fear are deep and can be traced to the fact that women have spent years and years feeling powerless to make enough money to support themselves on their own. If you don't feel you can make large amounts of money, you might always live with the fear of losing your money and being unable to replace it.

Men, on the other hand, have more limited fears, which may seem to be more "realistic" at first blush. They fear being unemployed, being injured at work, dying young and leaving a family with not enough money to support themselves.

It is important for women and men to try to empathize with the deep fears of the other sex, to find a way of supporting and reassuring each other that will lead to a lessening of anxiety around these imagined traumas.

Power, Control, and Decision Making in the Family

Men tend to wield the financial power in the home as well as the business world. Many women will gladly surrender this power to their male partners. In other households, the men will just assume the power, and the women will accept their subsidiary role—for a while, anyway. Studies seem to indicate that in families where men make more money than women, they control the finances in the majority of cases. And although, as we've seen, 20 percent of wives were making more money than their husbands in 1990, many therapists like myself have found that a good number of these women seem to be less comfortable with assuming financial control and authority on the basis of their income superiority. In my therapy practice through the years, I have found that often, even in families where the woman pays the bills and balances the checkbook, the major decisions about money and how it is spent still rest with the man. When we look at gay male couples, this difference persists: the person who makes more tends to control the money and the way it is spent. But in couple relationships between gay women, despite income disparity, there is more equality and democracy among the members when it comes to decision making and power in general. In my own clinical experience, I have found that more men than women are comfortable with assuming the role of chief decision maker and having primary control over the money.*

It is useful to remember that although many men may still be deciding how their family spends and invests (e.g., which car, computer, or CD player to buy; how much to put away for retirement

---

* Donald Katz, in "Men, Women, and Money: The Last Taboo," p. 59, speculates that women may be "less comfortable using money as an agent of control."

or for the kids' college fund; which stocks to invest in), in many cases it is the woman who is spending the discretionary income. She is likely to spend the money in smaller chunks than the man does, but her total expenditures may actually be greater. So the situation may not be as one-sided as it may appear.

If you are in a couple relationship, when you look at the conflicts with your partner over money, you need to determine whether there is a large power imbalance as far as controlling the money is concerned. If either one of you feels uncomfortable about this imbalance, try to move toward a more democratic distribution of power. In the following chapters, you will find tools to help you tackle this difficult area respectfully and safely.

Why do so many couples have such trouble with shared decision making? Even when both partners have comparable incomes, men's and women's styles of decision making tend to differ. A man in a couple relationship will tend to make decisions, even about large 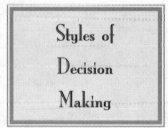 purchases, on his own, and will usually not consider the possibility of consulting his partner about such decisions. The woman, on the other hand, might enjoy consulting her mate about even small purchases, since it reinforces her sense of togetherness, of being a team. If a woman takes this male tendency toward unilateral decision making personally, rather than as an expression of men's perception of boundaries and autonomy, she will be hurt, angry, and may even feel betrayed by such "thoughtlessness" on the part of her man. The man, on the other hand, will feel controlled and constrained if his woman suggests that they make all decisions together; it's as if his mother is scolding him and telling him he has

Styles of Decision Making

to ask permission to buy that bigger computer or better CD player. Having to ask his partner about buying a new computer, or even a new family car, can make the man feel one-down or, in some cases, humiliated. This is another manifestation of the difference between men's view of the world as competitive and women's view as cooperative.

These attitudes are so ingrained that it is difficult to reverse them. But if men and women will begin to understand each other's "culture" and not take the differences between them so personally, they may well be able to negotiate agreements through structured moneytalks and goal-setting sessions (see chapters 10 and 11). Then, some decisions can be made by the man alone, in his comfortable, self-contained style; others will be made by the couple together, to honor many women's need for sharing and joint decision making; and still others can be made by the woman alone, if she chooses.

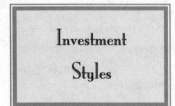

Investment Styles

In my money work with couples, I've noticed time and again that most men seem more willing to take risks with their money than women are. Why is this so? Women's long history of being financially dependent on men and of earning less money than men do may contribute to women's hesitation to risk much money when investing. Men's experience of mastery in higher-paying jobs and physical mastery in risk-taking situations may contribute to their readiness to take more risks with their money.

The most significant thing to understand about this difference is that for risk takers who tend to be men, the act of risk taking is experienced as freedom, excitement, and intense pleasure. For

risk-avoider women, the safety and security of conservative investments and other relatively safe financial choices feel like freedom and safety. On the other hand, when a risk avoider takes
risks with money, it feels dangerous, if not downright suicidal.
And when a risk taker avoids risks, it feels constraining and even
claustrophobic. For men and women who function in opposite
modes in this area to understand each other and to move toward
each other requires a high degree of openness and a willingness to experiment with the other's mode. (More about this in
chapter 7.)

When women choose financial advisers,
they tend to use a combination of rational linear thinking and intuitive decision making that places a heavy
emphasis on the quality of trust and
safety in the relationship. When "feeling type" women make mistakes in

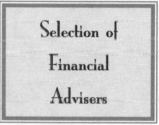

Selection of
Financial
Advisers

choosing financial advisers, they may be concentrating more on
whether they feel comfortable with the person they are hiring than
on the individual's financial track record, credentials, and experience. "Thinking type" men tend to choose financial advisers without asking themselves whether they feel safe or comfortable with
them. They typically use two methods of financial decision making.
The first involves a fairly rational "thinking type" process, finding
out about the company's performance, reputation, and so on. The
second method is to take action, either in choosing advisers or in
choosing investments on their own, based on tips from friends. His
method is often not rational at all but rather quite impulsive, and
may end up being at least as dangerous as women's more intuitive-
emotional mode. For financial experts tell me that one major way

in which men tend to lose money through investing is by taking large financial risks based on tips from friends.

Obviously, each style has its strengths and weaknesses. When couples join forces to choose experts, these styles may well be at cross-purposes. But if there is communication and cooperation, partners can learn from each other as well as help each other deal with chronic blind spots in this area. There needs to be a fair amount of trust and mutual respect in the relationship for men and women to be willing to open up enough to learn from each other in this way. In many relationships, though our partners have much to teach us, they are the last person we are willing to place in this mentor role. Learning to be each other's mentors is an ongoing process and is well worth the effort.

Styles of Philanthropic Giving

Men are likely to be competitive and women cooperative when they give to charity. In an article in *Lilith* magazine about the differences between Jewish men and women in their philanthropic styles,* it was noted that men tend to give to causes partly because their colleagues do, and that they often demonstrate their clout and power through the size of the contributions they make. So, although the men do give to causes they believe in, there seems to be an element of jockeying for power, of competing for status, in the way they give to charity. They also may tend to give in one fell swoop, without asking a lot of questions about where the money goes, or exactly how it will be used. Comedian Rob Becker might say, "They 'kill' the charity, in the same way they 'kill' the shirt on a shopping

---

* Susan Weidman Schneider, "Jewish Women's Philanthropy: What Do We Need to Know?" *Lilith*, Winter 1993, pp. 7–12, 29, 38, and 39.

trip!" Women, on the other hand, tend to be more private in their giving and gather much more information about the causes and charities they support. Are there women in this organization? Is there child care? Where does the money go? As they gather this information, women care about feeling emotionally connected to the causes they support. They are in general less concerned about how much their friends are giving, unless it is to give the same amount and thus feel more connected to their friends and joined in a cooperative effort of giving.

If couples are trying to decide together where and how to give, they need to learn to harmonize these different philanthropic styles. It is also important for them to accept each other's mode without judgment. (You can develop this skill by using the communication techniques I will teach you in chapter 8.)

When it comes to how the money is held by the couple, either in joint accounts or in separate ones, men and women tend to change places in terms of who wants to tear down boundaries and who wants to erect them. It is usually the man who wants to merge the

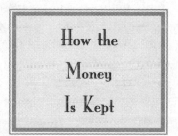

How the
Money
Is Kept

money, and the woman who wants some or all separate money. Explanations for these preferences are usually superficial or focus on the negative aspects of each person's desire. Thus, men will say to their women: "Why do you want separate money? You must not trust me!" Or: "Are you planning to divorce me? No? Well, then, why do you need separate money?" And women will counter angrily: "Why do you want to merge the money? You must want to control me!" There may indeed be grains of truth in each analysis, for men have typically assumed the provider/controller role, and women realize that in this age of skyrocketing divorce, they *will* get a lot poorer and their men a lot richer if they do divorce.*   Nevertheless, I believe that each is overlooking a deeper longing that is at work here. In fact, individual men and women often do not understand their own deeper needs around intimacy.

For the man, the main challenge of intimacy is to learn to merge, to get connected and stay connected. His wanting to merge the money may well be a loving expression of his desire for a fuller connection with his partner. On the other hand, a woman's primary challenge in intimate relationships is to learn how to preserve her healthy sense of autonomy in the midst of intimacy. Wanting some or all separate money is a symbol of this healthy separateness, enabling her to connect with her man from a deeper, more solid place.

Some couples, of course, do not fit this pattern: some find that both members want some or all separate money; and other couples merge all the money, and there seems to be no problem at all. But in relationships where there is some tension around this issue, understanding both men's and women's deeper needs can resolve the problem once and for all.

When we look at male-female differences in the areas of merged-versus-separate money, and risk taking versus risk avoidance, we see two major polarization patterns that are strongly linked to gender. In chapter 7, I will discuss these and other non-gender-related polarizations, to show you how to reach balance in all these areas. In this chapter, it is enough for you to understand the "cultural" differences that fuel these distinctions and preferences.

* In "Men, Women, and Money: The Last Taboo," Donald Katz states on p. 58 that "divorced husbands' standards of living tend to rise by 40%, whereas divorced women's incomes fall by an average of 70%."

WHAT KIND OF MONEYTALK
WILL WE HAVE?

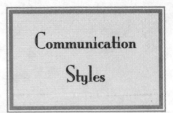

Communication Styles

Many men will often complain that their mates are unwilling to sit down and talk about the money. What "thinking type" men mean by this is that many women seem resistant to discussing the hard, concrete facts of the couple's finances. "Feeling type" women, on the other hand, complain about men's resistance to dealing with the couple's dynamics and both members' emotional reactions about money. So she wants to sit down and talk about the ways that the couple doesn't work together or doesn't share power, or discuss some of her yearnings about what to do with their money; and her partner wants to talk about the facts. How can the couple resolve this difference? As a psychotherapist (and perhaps also because I am clearly a "feeling type" woman), I have found that the best solution is for the couple to agree to talk feelings and dynamics first, and hard facts afterward. Only after feelings are resolved can the facts be aired and heard, and clear negotiations follow.

Even when both men and women have agreed to try and have a moneytalk, their disparate communication styles can lead to hurt, misunderstanding, and chronic conflict. Most women have a need to be empathetically heard and emotionally understood in these discussions. But when they share their feelings, men often feel burdened with unnecessary information. Or worse, they feel criticized and unaccepted. Many men like to look for quick, rational decisions, and to give advice and their own analysis of the situation (the hunter role again). When they act this way while women are trying to be heard and understood, and to "gather" all the different aspects of the issue to share, the women feel patronized, lectured at, and disrespected or ignored. These communication problems combine the major differences between men and women: hunter versus gatherer; competition versus cooperation; thinking type versus feeling type.*

WILL YOU LOOK AT ME OR NOT?

To further complicate attempts at communication, women view making eye contact with their men and either talking to them directly or touching them physically as signs of connectedness. Men, on the other hand, often feel close and most comfortable when not making eye contact; and when their women are merely around, in their orbit, and even on another floor of the house.

When men and women come together to have moneytalks, then, it is important to understand these differences and not take them personally. When you learn how to conduct structured moneytalks in chapters 8 through 10, you will be incorporating non-eye-contact communication (to help you share emotionally charged topics) and direct eye contact (to share positive thoughts and feelings).

WHO'S TO BLAME?

Earlier, we talked about many men's tendency to take credit and assign blame in the face of financial successes and failures. We also saw that for women, the tendency is to give credit elsewhere and to swallow blame for poor financial outcomes. Thus, when men and

---

* In *You Just Don't Understand: Women and Men in Conversation*, Deborah Tannen discusses many manifestations of these differences; see chapter 6, "Community and Contest: Styles in Conflict," pp. 149–87.

women have money conflicts with each other, the tendency is for the man to blame the woman, and for the woman to blame herself. Now in some families, angry fights will seem evenly matched, with both members trying to pin the blame on the other. With other couples, it is the woman who is actually more verbally "violent" and attacking; and the man is more physically explosive and abusive. But in many other cases, the dynamic will go like this: The man will say, "It's your fault we have no money; look at the crazy things you spend it on!" The woman will act defensive but will say to herself, "He's right; he makes most of the money, and I *am* a little reckless and impulsive." But the cycle will not end there. The woman, feeling blamed and wronged, will secretly (or not so secretly) begin harboring more and more resentment toward her mate for making her feel this way. She will ultimately get even with him in a variety of ways: being critical of his other weaknesses, acting cold and distant, withholding sex, or even spending more rebelliously, and more in secret. So unless both men and women can agree to minimize blame (and self-blame) and to focus on their own part of the dynamic (the only part that each has real control of, after all), they will stay locked in a hostile dynamic that will only escalate over time, leaving a trail of hurts, grudges, and resentments in its wake. (In chapters 8 through 10, you will get help in overcoming these destructive patterns.)

HEALING STYLES

When men and women are engaging in a moneytalk on a loaded topic, and they get hurt or angry, how do they react? The man will generally want to withdraw, to get some space to heal; as John Gray puts it, he needs "to go into his cave" for a while.* The woman

---

* John Gray, *Men Are from Mars, Women Are from Venus* (New York: HarperCollins, 1992), p. 31.

will want to talk the problem out right then and there. The only way to resolve this difference is for one person to surrender to the other's need temporarily. Either the woman will need to learn to tolerate giving her man a little space—it's helpful if the man is willing to say when he will be ready to come back to process the glitch—or the man will need to learn to hang in there and tolerate his emotional discomfort while the couple tries to resolve their problem. The partner who gets to use his or her habitual healing style should try to tell the other, "I realize and appreciate that you're doing something that makes you feel quite uncomfortable for the sake of our relationship."

Cultivating Compassion and Respect for Our Differences

How do we need to use all this information about male-female differences around money? By understanding and accepting these "cultural" differences with curiosity and compassion, rather than with threats and judgments, we create a climate of mutual respect and interest, in which we are able to figure out how to make financial decisions to-gether and how to talk about our money in a way that minimizes conflict, tension, and misunderstanding.

The importance of cultivating compassion and respect for our differences will also be discussed in the next chapter, when we look at the major patterns of polarization that couples exhibit in connection with money.

7.

Couples Polarization Patterns:

Resolving Power Struggles and

Moving Toward the Middle

In many cases, when we look around at couple relationships among our friends and reflect on our own relationships, we find that "opposites attract" right off the bat. Introverts choose extroverts; wild-and-free types select super-responsible types; verbal types pick nonverbal types; people who like to hang out and rest choose partners who are more active in the world; and on and on. When it comes to money, tightwads marry spendthrifts, worriers marry avoiders, planners marry dreamers, and on and on. And often, even when opposites don't attract, they will be created eventually. If two spenders marry, for example, they will fight each other for the superspender role, and the loser will begin to "hoard" by comparison. This polarizing "dance," it seems to me, is in most cases inevitable.

Over time, these polarizations tend to become more rigid and conflict ridden for many couples. Each partner attacks the other for his or her habitual stance or failings. So the spender, who at first admired his hoarder mate's skills with budgeting and financial planning, now accuses her of being stingy and obsessed with petty details. The hoarder, in turn, changes her assessment of her partner's free-and-easy style of spending: what was once seen as spontaneous and generous behavior is now considered irresponsible, immature, and selfish.

In this chapter, we will be looking at the most common polarizations of money personality styles and determining what can be done to harmonize these differences. Here are the major polarizations I have found:

Hoarder versus Spender
Planner versus Dreamer
Money Worrier versus Money Avoider
Money Monk versus Money Amasser
Money Merger versus Money Separatist
Risk Taker versus Risk Avoider

More general polarization patterns that affect a couple's moneylife together are:

Victim versus Victimizer
Goal Setter A versus Goal Setter B

We will spend some time exploring each major polarizing "dance." As you read about these patterns, try to identify which ones you demonstrate in your own couple relationship. You may even discover that you are one money type in your couple relationship, another type with your children, and still another type with your parents or with the boss at work. Once you've identified your own major polarizations, I will give you the tools to begin the harmonizing process of depolarization in *any* relationship.

Hoarders tend to save, budget, prioritize, and delay gratification. Money is
viewed as security, primarily. Hoarders
enjoy saving money and have a hard
time spending money on anyone
(themselves included). Spenders, on

the other hand, enjoy using their money to bring pleasure to themselves and others. They tend to be more spontaneous, generous,
impulsive, and, if they are extreme spenders, can be somewhat out
of control in their spending patterns.

The old stereotype is that hoarder men are married to spender
women. (Comics have had a field day with this one!) But even if
this stereotype used to have any truth in it, it certainly doesn't
anymore. As increasing numbers of women enter the workforce and
take on greater responsibility for their finances, some of them are
more likely to function as hoarders in their couple relationship.
And as I mentioned earlier, even if you don't start out in a polarization with your partner, one will probably evolve over time. So if
two hoarders join forces, they will fight each other for the super-
hoarder role, and the loser will learn to spend by comparison. It is
extremely rare to see two members of a couple who are both happy
hoarders, or happy spenders, with no polarizing tensions at all.
(Not impossible—but rare!)

A HOARDER-SPENDER MARRIAGE:
DAN AND SONDRA

Dan and Sondra had been married for fifteen years. They had been
high school sweethearts. Dan came from a wealthy family that had
lost everything in the Depression. He was a corporate executive
whose earnings increased every year, and he held on to his money

for dear life, afraid of losing it as his father had. He was an extreme hoarder. Sondra came from a working-class family that had just started to make good, and had given up her job as a schoolteacher to stay home and raise their two children. When they entered therapy, Dan complained bitterly that Sondra's shopaholic tendencies would send them to the poorhouse. Sondra told me tearfully, "He's a cheapskate who won't even buy his kids the clothing they need to fit in with their friends at school." She went on to further expose her husband's limitations, telling me in a voice laced with smoldering resentment which covered over her hurt: "All he cares about is money. Why, for our fifteenth anniversary, all he bought me was a crummy record. Can you imagine!" Dan was stupefied. He countered, equally hurt: "I took hours off from work for three days in a row to look for that record. It was the song we danced to at our senior prom, when I asked her to go steady. And that's how she appreciates all my efforts!"

For Dan, money equaled security. For Sondra, money equaled love. So every time he saved money, he felt happy and she felt deprived. Every time she spent money, she felt happy and he felt anxious and fearful. Only by beginning to understand each other's world and trying on aspects of each other's money style could these warring mates begin to harmonize their differences.

Through the course of therapy, Dan looked at the limitations of his excessive hoarding, and Sondra recognized the rebellious aspects of her spending tendencies. Dan could finally admit that he admired Sondra's ability to give herself and her loved ones gifts and to enjoy life in the moment. And Sondra could acknowledge that she admired Dan's ability to set priorities and delay gratification for future goals and to ensure financial security. They also learned to conduct respectful moneytalks, even about difficult subjects. (See chapter 10 for one of these structured moneytalks.)

When Dan and Sondra admitted out loud what they secretly admired about the other's tendency to spend or hoard, they were taking an important step toward depolarization: *acknowledging secret envies and appreciations of your partner's money style.* But why don't couples do this more? Dan feared that in admitting to Sondra that he admired her generosity and ability to give, she would feel she had more license to go out and spend more wildly. And Sondra feared that if she told Dan she admired his ability to set priorities and to delay gratification, she'd be giving him permission to rein her in more tightly. Actually, when they stopped attacking each other for their faults, and instead complimented each other for their strengths, Sondra felt safe enough to admit that she'd like to learn more self-discipline, as Dan had; and Dan was free to admit that he'd like to loosen up and enjoy life with Sondra and the kids more, and not be so obsessed with saving vast amounts of money. Giving each other the benefit of the doubt can work wonders for any couple that is locked into a polarization.

Planners love to ponder the ins and outs of purchases and other financial expenditures. They dislike making spontaneous or impulsive decisions about money. They tend to think concretely and often are also hoarders who enjoy budgeting, prioritizing, and saving. Dreamers are future-oriented, passionate people who enjoy fantasizing about grand schemes and all the ways they can express their creativity and full potential in their moneylife. They generally dislike planning things out in minute detail, or at least find it very difficult to indulge in such activities.

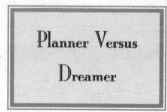

Planner Versus Dreamer

A PLANNER-DREAMER
COUPLE: KATE AND MARK

Several years ago, Mark and Kate had a few money therapy sessions with me and my original partner in this work. Mark was a dreamer in his midlife-crisis years. He wanted to quit his $60,000-a-year corporate job and begin teaching emotionally disturbed kids in a special school he'd heard about. Kate was a planner, the nitty-gritty detail person in the family. She had just completed her course work for a graduate degree and was about to write her final thesis in order to complete the program. She had never worked outside their home. They had one daughter, Emily, who had finished her first year of college. Kate was panicked that her dreamer husband would quit his job in a fit of frustration and try to teach in that special school he kept talking about, which paid $20,000 a year for beginners in the field. She could imagine doom and destruction for the family: they would have to sell their house; Emily would have to drop out of school when the money ran out; and many other disasters would arise.

My colleague and I gave them a simple assignment that represents another step in the depolarization process: *learning to move toward the middle*. Every week for three weeks, Mark had to act like the planner—making concrete and detailed plans about how he could make this job transition without throwing the family into chaos and crisis. Kate had to let herself fantasize and dream—about herself first, before moving on to family fantasies—about all the things she yearned to do in her life. They both were asked to write down all their feelings about their new behaviors. Within a week or two, they reported having the most intimate and fruitful conversations of their long married life. After three weeks (and a total of three, two-hour therapy sessions), they had completed the entire process of depolarization.

Mark and Kate came up with a most creative solution to their family dilemma. Through Kate's writing down her yearnings, they both discovered a shared dream to live abroad or travel abroad. Mark realized that his company had a branch office in Belgium, and they agreed that he would ask for a transfer for two years. He got the transfer, was paid the same salary, and during their stay there, Kate completed her graduate thesis. In the summer Mark took courses in special education, to see how he liked the field. In the meantime, their daughter, Emily, completed her third year of college. When they returned from Belgium two years later, Kate had her advanced degree and could begin earning more money, and Mark was pursuing a whole new career path.

I don't know whether Mark's new job paid more than $20,000 per year or not; I respected their privacy when the couple called to tell me their good news. But I do know that they both seemed happy and excited about the course of their lives at that point. Because each one moved toward the middle in their simple assignments, they could make decisions as a couple that satisfied both parties.

Money worriers tend to obsess or worry about money all the time. They may spend a lot of time poring over their checkbook, making sure their budget is still okay, thinking about possible investments. Avoiders try not to focus on any aspect of their moneylife any

Money Worrier Versus Money Avoider

more than they absolutely have to. They avoid balancing their checkbook, doing taxes, paying bills, budgeting, and planning. Money worriers need a rest from too much obsessive concern about money; and money avoiders need to focus on money more, so they can face the realities of their moneylife and not feel so overwhelmed when it comes to dealing with their money and making financial decisions.

Barbara and Gordon were both in their second marriage and had been together for two years, married only a year, when they came to see me. Barbara's first marriage had been brief, and she had no children. She and her first husband had kept their money separate and had made about the same annual salary—$30,000 a year each. Gordon had been married to his first wife for twenty years and was paying her alimony and child support for their three sons. The twins, Bob and Mike, were just graduating from college, and the youngest son, Jeff, was just starting at a prestigious (and expensive) college during the first year of Gordon's new marriage. Barbara admitted she was something of a worrier, though she had never been so anxious about money as she was since marrying Gordon. Gordon was a doctor in a small practice, so he made a substantial income. But he was a chronic money avoider. He avoided billing patients on time, neglected to collect bills, paid taxes late every year, and all his disposable income was now used to cover Jeff's college costs and to keep up his agreements with his former wife and family. Barbara complained bitterly that Gordon was doing nothing financially to express his love and support for his new relationship with her. Moreover, he was expecting her to be loving and supportive toward his kids, and not to have any wants or needs of her own till Jeff was through with college.

In worrier-avoider marriages such as Barbara and Gordon's,

polarization can become severe if one person enters the marriage as an extreme type. If a worrier marries, his or her mate will become an avoider, since being around that much worry and tension will create money avoidance. If, on the other hand, an avoider enters a marriage, the other will become more of a worrier, since someone has to be concerned about the realities of the couple's financial life. In this case, Gordon's extreme avoidance of dealing with his moneylife and his tendency to overspend on his first family had intensified Barbara's previously mild tendency to worry about money. Since their marriage, she had become a full-fledged money worrier and more of a hoarder than ever before.

During therapy, both spouses wrote money dialogues and practiced nonhabitual behaviors. Gordon agreed to take on tasks he usually avoided, such as billing patients and collecting from them, and doing taxes on time; Barbara practiced intense short periods of "conscious worrying" so she could give it up more and more. After three months, their communication had improved and so had their relationship around money. Gordon could acknowledge how supportive his new wife was being in living frugally and using her money for the couple's needs while his youngest son was in college. And Barbara could acknowledge that Gordon's responsible behavior toward all three of his sons reflected a family loyalty that also extended to her as his new wife. His loving gestures of writing her cards to express his gratitude for her help in supporting his son in college made her feel more appreciated in the relationship. And his progress in collecting fees and keeping records up-to-date made her feel more secure.

If you and your partner are stuck in avoider-worrier dynamics, don't panic. This is one of the most common polarizing dances, and with a little effort and goodwill, you can make progress in turning this dynamic around.

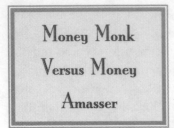

Money monks believe that money is evil and has the power to corrupt one's values and sense of personal integrity. They prefer being on the "have-not" end of the spectrum rather than becoming an evil "have." "Poverty consciousness" (i.e., living frugally and being supersensitive to the misfortunes of others) is seen as virtuous and amassing wealth as greedy and selfish. Money monks feel anxious and guilty if too much money comes to them, through salary increases, inheritance, or their spouse's winning the lottery. Money amassers, on the other hand, believe that money equals power and/ or self-worth, but in a positive sense. They believe that the more money they have to spend, to save, to invest, the better their life will be and the better they'll feel about themselves. So money monks think that money is bad for you, and money amassers think that nothing could be finer than to have a lot of money. You can see how a marriage or relationship between a money monk and a money amasser will be fraught with tension and gaps in understanding each other's universe.

A MONEY MONK–MONEY AMASSER MARRIAGE: DEVON AND KAREN

Devon and Karen had been married for five years and were both in their early thirties. They first met while marching in a civil rights demonstration. Devon worked for an environmental group and earned $25,000 a year. Karen had finished law school right before they met and was working for a small law firm that specialized in affirmative-action cases and women's issues. She made $45,000 a year and was about to get a large raise in the next few months. Devon came from a working-class Catholic family of eight children. Karen came from an upper-middle-class family and had two older brothers. One was a doctor and the other an electrical engineer.

The tension in Devon and Karen's marriage centered on vacations and on whether to buy a new car. Devon was a money monk who was determined to live a life of simplicity and never to become like the "fat cats" he loathed. He owned an old Volkswagen Beetle that was falling apart, and drove around in it with pride. Though Karen was politically liberal and activist, she liked the fact that she was making more and more money every year; she wanted to take a vacation in the Caribbean and maybe even buy herself a Honda Accord with some of the money from her raise. Devon looked on these desires of Karen's as "disgustingly bourgeois."

How did this couple resolve their differences? The challenge for money monks and amassers, and for any other pair of opposites, for that matter, is to change places and perspectives to some degree. This reversal of roles and/or perspectives is only temporary; but it can go a long way toward building empathy for your partner's position and loosening up your own biases and rigidities when it comes to your moneylife. Both Devon and Karen were willing to search for examples that ran counter to their own prejudices, or perhaps I should say biases. Devon was able to loosen up his contemptuous judgments of those with wealth by finding people around him (and in the media) who were wealthy and were doing wonderful things with their money, in his opinion. He even found examples of those who were bettering the world with their money as well as having some fun with it. Karen located examples of people without a lot of money who were living happy and full lives. Devon and Karen also gained insight into their own emotional loads around money and learned to communicate with each other about their past histories with money (see chapter 9 for Devon and

Karen's structured moneytalk); thus, each partner began to have more empathy for the other's feelings and desires. Slowly, Devon could tolerate Karen giving herself some pleasures of life without disrespecting her for her choices. And Karen could let Devon preserve a certain style of living that was more spartan than the one she would have chosen for herself. Clinical researchers Howard J. Markman and Clifford Notarius, who have spent years examining happily married versus distressed couples, report that it is not the degree of difference between the members of a couple which determines their degree of marital contentment, but how they sit with these differences.* In learning to communicate more effectively and empathetically about their differences, Devon and Karen learned to accept them, and to work with them more creatively.

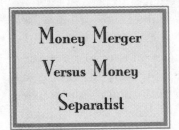

Money Merger Versus Money Separatist

Money mergers want to merge the money in couple relationships; money separatists want to keep some or all of it in separate accounts. Sometimes, of course, both people are mergers, or both are separatists, and then there is no tension; the money is either merged or kept totally separate. Old married couples sometimes come up to me after presentations and say: "Very interesting what you said about joint and separate money. But we've always put everything together, and it seems to work perfectly for us." But in cases where one partner is a merger and the other is a separatist, hurt feelings and misunderstandings can easily arise.

---

* "Controlling the Fires of Marital Conflict: Constructive and Destructive Strategies to Manage Anger," by Clifford I. Notarius and Howard J. Markman, presented at the Maryland Psychological Association/Foundation 1990–91 Postdoctoral Institute Workshop, December 7, 1990, in Columbia, Maryland.

I have found in my work with couples through the years that with this polarization pattern, it is most often the woman who wants some or all separate money, and the man who wants to merge the money. If the couple gets locked into a negative mode around this difference, and each partner accuses the other of base motivations, they will both end up feeling hurt and angry. But if they can develop some understanding of each other's deeper needs in terms of intimacy patterns, they will be able to work in harmony toward finding a mutually satisfying solution to this problem. (For more details on this topic, turn back to the discussion in chapter 6.)

A MERGER-SEPARATIST CONFLICT:
ANDREW AND JULIA

When I appeared on a television show and talked about couples conflicts over money, a young man named Andrew stood up to ask me a question. "I'm engaged to be married," he said, his eyes blazing with anger, "and I'm already having trouble with Julia, my fiancée, about our money. Why is it always 'her' money or 'our' money? That is so unfair! And what is this 'her money' about anyway?!" I explained to Andrew that men and women have different challenges in learning to be intimate. For men, the hard task is learning to get connected and stay connected. Thus, for many men, a desire to merge the money reflects this longing for more togetherness and connection in the relationship. For women, on the other hand, connection usually comes naturally; what is difficult is learning not to lose themselves in the relationship. Thus, many women's desire to have some or all separate money reflects a longing for healthy autonomy in the midst of intimacy.

As I shared my reflections with Andrew, the anger in his eyes disappeared, and he looked softer and more empathetic as he talked about his bride-to-be. "What you're saying makes sense," he said. "Now maybe we can work out what to do with our money—and Julia's!" I reminded him that if he wanted some separate money in the name of fairness and equality, that was fine, too. But solutions don't have to look symmetrical to work for a couple. They just need to respect each individual's deeper psychological needs, for both healthy independence and healthy interdependence.

DEALING WITH A DISPARITY IN INCOME: GLORIA AND ERIC

Whenever there are vast differences in the amount of money that each person brings to the couple relationship, I think it is important for partners to discuss openly how they feel about this disparity. In the same vein, I recommend that they talk about who pays for what, and whether the money will be kept separately or together.

Men have historically been the primary breadwinners, so they have tended to be the ones making much larger salaries than their mates. Many of these men may want to merge the money because they believe that in their traditional role as *chief* provider this is the way a "good husband" operates (as well as to express an unconscious desire for intimacy, as we have discussed). But today we see an increasing number of couples in which the woman makes more money than her mate. For some couples, this situation is not a loaded issue. For others, one or both partners feel uncomfortable about it.

Gloria, a woman who makes twice the salary of her husband, Eric, shared with me her personal feelings on the subject. She con-

fessed that she didn't like to be constantly reminded that she made
so much more than her spouse, but she did think it was fair for her
to pay more for household expenses, rent, and the like. So Gloria
and Eric came up with a creative solution that was working well
for them. "At the beginning of the month," she said, "we put
money into a couples fund for joint expenses. I put in twice as much
money as Eric does. Then, during the month, we take everything
we need out of that pool. I know to put in $1,000 every month, and
I know that Eric contributes only $500. But now that this is our
habit, I don't have to keep remembering every minute that I'm
paying twice as much as Eric is for our joint expenses. The system
works perfectly, and I'm proud of us for coming up with it." (I
think such a system would have worked just as well if Eric had
been the one earning the higher salary.)

As I explained in chapter 6, risk takers
like the thrill and the adventure that
high risk with money provides. Risk
avoiders are conservative investors who
prefer holding on to their money and
being sure they will not risk losing it.

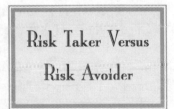

Risk takers tend to be dreamers; risk avoiders tend to be planners.
Risk takers are often spenders, and risk avoiders are often hoarders; but this is not always the case. Some of my female clients have
complained to me about their overspending tendencies in general;
but when they are investing their money, they will avoid risk at all
costs. As I noted earlier, this polarization, and the preceding one
around merging and separation of money, are the only two that
seem to be largely based on gender.

When it comes to the degree of risk that people prefer, one
person's hell is often another's heaven. Risking a substantial

amount of money makes the risk taker feel alive and free with no boundaries; it makes the risk avoider feel terrified, just *because* there are no boundaries. Avoiding high risks with money causes the risk taker to feel constrained, as if in a straitjacket; it causes the risk avoider to feel safe, secure, and free—free from anxiety and fear, that is.

A RISK TAKER—RISK AVOIDER MARRIAGE: ALAN AND EILEEN

Alan, a corporate executive, was a high risk taker when it came to investing his money. His wife, Eileen, was extremely conservative with the money she made as the manager of a large department store. One day, without saying a word to his wife, Alan invested a large chunk of money in futures—and lost it all. This loss threw a monkey wrench into the family finances, and eventually he could no longer keep the news from his wife. When Alan finally confessed, Eileen was at first in shock; then she felt angry and betrayed. In a gesture of shamefaced reconciliation, Alan agreed to let his wife handle all their money for the next couple of years.

But after a year had gone by, and they were slowly recovering from their financial crisis, the couple came to me for therapy because Alan was feeling like a prisoner in his own home with regard to money. Slowly, with me, they were each able to look at their extreme tendencies in the area of risk. They began to understand what it felt like to be inside their partner's skin. And they negotiated a new agreement: (1) Eileen would still be in charge of a large chunk of the family's money, but Alan would take back a piece of it to spend as he saw fit. (2) They would have periodic meetings about money, in which they would share what was going on in an open and respectful way. (3) They would invest a small portion of their money in investments that constituted a larger risk than Eileen's choices of the past year. (4) Alan would attend several meetings of Gamblers Anonymous, to see if he could benefit from the free group support he might find there. Having moved toward the middle, Alan and Eileen were on their way to healing the psychological wounds of their financial crisis.

If you are truly willing to "walk a mile in your partner's moccasins" (or even a quarter of a mile!) in spite of the temporary feelings of discomfort that this causes, the rewards will be tremendous in terms of creativity, flexibility, and intimacy with your mate.

When one person assumes the role of the powerful victimizer, and the other takes on the complementary role of the powerless victim, the polarizing struggle can become laced with hostility and even, in the extreme, with violence. The

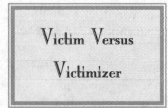

Victim Versus
Victimizer

story of Michael and Jennifer is all too common. Michael earned a much larger salary than Jennifer, and she let him handle all the money and make all the decisions for years. At the beginning of their relationship he said, "Don't worry your pretty head about this," and she was happy to let him attend to the financial details. But as the years wore on, and Jennifer had to ask Michael for money all the time and justify her purchases to him, she began expressing her resentment that he controlled the money: She would refuse to have sex, or attack Michael verbally, or even secretly skim money to get even with him.

For every stereotypical example of a "macho man" who controls the money, there is an example of a woman who chooses to stay powerless and uninformed rather than take on the hard and

scary work of self-education and self-empowerment about finances. But as women begin making more money, we see a reversal
of the stereotype of the controlling husband versus the powerless,
resentful wife. Recently, I read about a woman who made most of
the money in a marriage and called all of the financial shots. She
even dictated where and when the couple would go on vacation,
where they would stay, and so on. Her husband's response to this
imbalance was to refuse to have sex with her.* When these
"power plays" and "paybacks" exist,† if nothing is done to
change the pattern, the relationship will end in divorce or will be
characterized by chronic resentment, hostility, and punishment.

A VICTIM—VICTIMIZER
COUPLE: JOYCE AND GLEN

One of the most horrifying examples of what can happen in a relationship devastated by power plays is that of Joyce and Glen. Joyce
was a caller who phoned in to the "Oprah Winfrey Show" while I
was appearing as a guest. She told us that her husband, Glen, had
been very controlling about money for many years. One day she
decided that she would no longer tolerate feeling so straitjacketed
by him and so financially and emotionally deprived. So she began
skimming money and squirreling it away. But Joyce wouldn't leave
it at that. She got so good at being sneaky that when she found a
way to begin using other people's credit card numbers to get the
things she wanted, she developed that skill into a high art form.

---

* This example was quoted from a case study by psychiatrist Ann Ruth Turkel in the *Journal of the American Academy of Psychoanalysis*, in Don Katz's article "Men, Women, and Money: The Last Taboo," *Worth*, June 1993, p. 59.

† Victoria Felton-Collins uses these terms in her book *Couples and Money: Why Money Interferes with Love and What to Do About It*, which she wrote with Suzanne Blair Brown (New York, Bantam rack edition, 1992); see chapter 3, "Power Plays, Paybacks, and Other Bad Investments," pp. 51–70.

She had been stealing in this way for years, and she was hatching a plan to pin the blame on Glen if she ever got caught. Watching our show about couples polarization patterns, she had glimmers of awareness that maybe this pseudosolution wasn't working as well for her as she thought. She did have more things as a result; but she felt more and more shaky about herself and more hateful toward Glen. I remember feeling temporarily overwhelmed by Joyce's confession, but Oprah came right back with her amazing blend of humor and compassion, and somehow found the right words to acknowledge the seriousness of Joyce's situation without making her feel too terrible to consider making a change in her illegal and dangerous behavior.

Though not all situations are as extreme as this one, all of us would do well to consider the ways in which we perpetuate power struggles in our own relationships, by controlling information, hoarding power, keeping secrets, or resorting to behaviors motivated by old grudges, rebellion, lack of trust, and lack of openness. The more we are willing to look at our own part in keeping these power struggles going, the clearer we will be about how to change them.

Goal Setter A Versus Goal Setter B

Sometimes, polarization is simply a matter of having different priorities and goals about what you'd like to do with your money. If this is so, you can reach a compromise with your partner whereby you each get a piece of what you want. Or, if you understand the longings that underlie your goals, you may even discover that alternate goals would be just as satisfying to you—and one of them may not be in conflict with your partner's goals at all.

A CONFLICT OVER BUYING A
HOUSE: JACK AND LENA

Jack and Lena came to me squabbling about their goals. She wanted to buy a house, which represented to her both being financially secure and "having arrived" in some sense. Jack, however, vehemently opposed such a purchase. His father had spent his whole life working at a job he hated just so he could make house payments on a mortgage that was basically more than he could afford. Jack had vowed never to get trapped in this way. Although Jack and Lena's problem appeared insoluble at first, when they began to explore their underlying feelings, they discovered that they might very well be able to accommodate each other's desires. After realizing that all his negative feelings about owning a home were attributable to his father's trauma, Jack was able to start thinking about buying a small home that wouldn't rule out his other spending options and goals. And Lena could now begin to look for ways to feel financially secure and successful other than through home ownership. The more they each understood their own motivations, the more easily they could come up with several solutions that might work well for them. (In chapter 11, you will learn about the most effective ways for you and your partner to fulfill individual and mutual goals.)

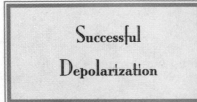

Successful

Depolarization

Depolarization is accomplished through a combination of the following:

- Communicating openly and honestly with your partner.

- Acknowledging secret envies and appreciations of your partner's money style.
- Learning to "move toward the middle" by practicing the behaviors and attitudes that are hardest for you.
- Monitoring your emotional reactions to these new behaviors and attitudes.
- Rewarding yourself for taking positive action.

When a couple has successfully depolarized, this doesn't mean that the hoarder has become a quasi spender, and the spender has become a quasi hoarder. It does mean that the couple does not experience chronic tension between these two opposing modes. It means that the hoarder has probably loosened up his or her tendency to save or hold on to money at all costs, and that the spender has the choice of sometimes saving money, prioritizing for long-term goals, and sticking to a spending plan, when he or she commits to one.

I recently met a man named Maury, who was definitely a hoarder and a worrier, compared to his wife, Evelyn, who was the spender and the avoider. After many happy years of marriage, they had worked out a way to live with each other's styles and accept each other's differences. Maury's tone of voice when he joked with me exhibited a loving acceptance of what he considered to be his wife's spending quirks. He said, "I used to say that the way we divided up the money I made in the restaurant business was to throw the money up to the ceiling; whatever stayed up there was mine; whatever came back down was hers!" Though this statement might give the impression that Maury was like a lot of older, traditional men who complain about their wife's tendencies to take all their hard-earned money and spend it, his light and loving tone, and the other ways he talked about his wife and his pride in her work and in her many talents, showed me that this couple had achieved a fair degree of money harmony. With all our imperfections and imbalances, if we have the proper degree of empathy and respect for our partner's strengths and weaknesses, and our own, we can all move toward this goal.

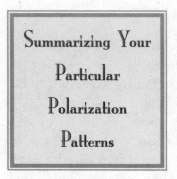

Summarizing Your Particular Polarization Patterns

Now that you have read about most of the ways that couples polarize over their differences, take some time to complete the following statements:

∗ Our most significant polarization is . . .

∗ Our second most significant dichotomy is . . .

∗ Our third most significant area of struggle is . . .
Optional. Two polarizations might be responsible for most of your money conflicts.

∗ I estimate that the percentage of money conflicts we have in each of these major areas is . . .
Example: 60 percent of conflicts are hoarder-spender battles; 30 percent are worrier-avoider conflicts; 10 percent are fights about different goals.

∗ For each polarization we manifest, I estimate that the degree of polarization, on a scale of 1 to 5, is . . .
Example: If 1 is the least extreme form and 5 is the most extreme, I would say that I am a 4-spender and my husband is a 2-hoarder. (So my behavior is more extreme than my husband's.)

Don't share these estimates with each other yet; and don't be wedded to these numbers. They are merely a reflection of your own perceptions about these differences in money style.

Here are a series of exercises that you and your partner can perform to help resolve the polarizations that are a source of conflict in your life together.

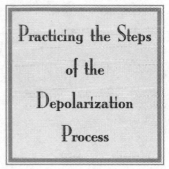

Practicing the Steps of the Depolarization Process

§ Acknowledge secret envies and appreciations of your partner's money style. Try to be as open, honest, and vulnerable with your partner as you can tolerate being.

§ Admit to your partner one way you would like to be more like him or her. You can write down your response first and share verbally afterward, or simply tell your partner directly—whatever works best for both of you.

§ For each polarization, select an assignment that will "move you toward the middle," that is, move you closer to your partner's style. It can be a new action, attitude, or behavior. Make a written list of these assignments, and tell your partner about them. Do the first assignment in the next week if possible (otherwise in the next few weeks or within a month). And allow a comfortable time interval between assignments so you can feel the full impact of each one.

§ Monitor your reactions to these assignments.

§ Reward yourself for performing each assignment. You might consider both an individual reward and a couples reward if you take on these tasks together.

What are the main things you learned from doing these exercises? What did you appreciate about this work? Take a few moments to jot down or notice what the depolarization process has meant for you. It's also a good idea to acknowledge your efforts in taking on such difficult and complicated issues and making some progress toward resolving them.

To continue along this road, you will learn, in the next chapter, some specific techniques that will facilitate better, more respectful communication with your partner.

8.

Couples Communication Techniques: Developing a Climate of Respect

We all know that when the members of a couple are screaming at each other, they are certainly not communicating effectively. And when one partner is lecturing while the other sits in stony silence, that's not effective communication either. Nor are conversations laced with criticisms and blame. In my twenty years of specializing in couples therapy, I've seen these and many other styles of ineffective communication that upset both parties and do not bring them one step closer to resolving the issues that separate them. Over and over again, I've noticed that couples simply do not have the skills to discuss highly charged topics—or, in some cases, even less emotional ones—in a way that allows them to listen with respect and respond with empathy, to negotiate calmly and rationally, and to make practical and mutually satisfying decisions together.

In this chapter, you will learn the general guidelines and specific techniques that I've taught my clients over the years so they

can talk with their mates in a respectful manner that brings positive results.* These skills can be applied to conversations you engage in with other people in your life as well, but our focus, in the
following chapters, will be on talks with your partner about money
and about shared and separate goals. Let's begin by establishing a
safe emotional climate.

Guidelines for Creating a Positive Emotional Climate

* *Even before you start communicating, think about what would
constitute practicing the nonhabitual for you.* Here's how my husband and I did this. I noted that I often began a conversation on a
thorny issue between us by complaining, blaming, and attacking him
for something he did that hurt me or made me angry. I tended to
explode at him in anger, which only made him back away and shut
down. To react in a new way for me meant focusing on my softer,
more vulnerable feelings of hurt; and taking care *not* to express blame
or anger toward my spouse. I could *feel* this anger, but I could choose
not to express it in this chronic way. On the other hand, since my
spouse's tendency was *not* to express negative feelings but rather to

* In the development of my couples communication techniques, I have been primarily influenced by
the following experts: Isaiah Zimmerman, a clinical psychologist in Washington, D.C., created a structured communication technique he called the "Format," which I have used and adapted in my couples
therapy for more than twenty years. (I will be teaching parts of it to you in this chapter.) In his excellent
article "Why Love Fails," Don Montagna, head of the Washington Ethical Society, outlines the power-
struggle phase of relationships and paves the way for what he calls "no-fault love." His conceptual
view parallels my own quite closely. Thomas Gordon's *P.E.T. Parent Effectiveness Training* stresses the
importance of using "I-messages" to minimize blame and "dumping" in communications. Lillian Rubin,
Deborah Tannen, John Gray, and Warren Farrell have many interesting and important things to say
about male-female differences.
  And finally, John Gray and Harville Hendrix have developed some valuable couples therapy techniques. Hendrix's way of looking at couple relationships is very close to my own: namely, that the two
members of a couple can help heal each other's early psychological minds over time, while doing the
work necessary to heal themselves individually. See the Bibliography for titles of works by these authors.

withdraw in silence when upset, choosing to *express* these angry feelings verbally was practicing the nonhabitual for him. Even though I didn't love having anger directed at me, it was refreshing to get a new reaction for a change! And my husband's way of expressing anger was controlled and respectful, which also helped me accept it.

* *Look at your own glitches first, instead of focusing on what your partner needs to do differently.* Practice saying, "I'm sorry I did that; I'll try to do better next time"—and meaning it—instead of lapsing into defensive explanations of your behavior. If your partner is upset at you for something you've said or done, and you are sure that the intensity of the reaction can be traced to older wounds in your mate that predate your relationship, acknowledge the part that you *did* play in upsetting your partner in the present, whether you meant to or not. Give him or her the space to tend to old wounds after you have helped heal the present one.

* *Practice looking at the positive qualities of your relationship, and of your partner.* Accentuating the positive will leave you with a lot more energy to deal with the negative.

* *Assume that win-win solutions are possible, even when you disagree.* If you and your partner take the time and effort to communicate your underlying needs and feelings, and hear each other with empathy and compassion, you will find, in most cases, that your needs may be different but not necessarily in direct conflict.*

---

* In *Getting to Yes: Negotiating Agreement Without Giving In* (New York: Penguin, 1983), Roger Fisher and William Ury give two famous examples of win-win solutions. In the first, two daughters are fighting over an orange. The mother, tired and rushed, cuts the orange in half and gives each daughter one-half. Both are unsatisfied. Why? Because one wanted the skin of the orange to make an orange cake, and the other wanted to eat the pulp. If the mother had taken the time and energy to ask each daughter what she wanted the orange for, she could have given each one exactly what they wanted. The second example describes a situation in a library. One man asks the librarian if he can open the window near him, because it's hot and stuffy. The other man, seated near him, complains of a draft. The librarian, in true win-win style, closes that window, and opens another one far away, which gives the first man the breeze he wants and avoids annoying his neighbor. Both examples show us that when we probe deeply enough into each other's needs, wants, and motivations, new solutions arise that can often satisfy two parties' seemingly divergent needs.

❧ *Minimize blame by using "I-messages" whenever possible.* In general, talk about your own feelings, instead of focusing on your partner's behavior or guessing at his or her negative motivations. For example, if you're bothered by your spouse's habit of leaving the room without saying good-bye to you, try saying, "When you leave the room without saying good-bye, I feel hurt; I feel ignored; I feel as if I don't exist; I feel rejected." Don't say, "I feel that you are an insensitive schmuck for leaving the room without saying good-bye to me!" The second remark is *not* an "I-message," though it uses the "I" form. It's a blaming judgment that will only be met with defensiveness and counterattack.

❧ *Practice hearing and repeating what your partner communicates to you—before launching into your own emotional reactions.* If you slow down the communication in this way, it will help both of you feel closer and more connected, and prevent you from getting into old, chronic patterns of attack and counterattack, or blame and defend.

❧ *Before you give the details of your communication, think about the nature of the message you will be sending, and announce it to your partner. If you are upset, see if your partner is willing to hear your feelings.* Let's say you are feeling stirred up, hurt, or angry. You could tell your partner, "I'm feeling upset about something," instead of immediately launching into a long exposition of what is upsetting you. Giving your mate this respectful warning will go a long way toward clarifying the communication. Asking if your partner is willing to listen also demonstrates that you respect his or her psychic space as well as take responsibility for your own feelings.

❧ *When your partner opens up to you and shares sensitive facts or feelings, receive that sharing as a gift.* Despite how tempting it might be to say things like, "Now I understand why you're so weird in that way," make a commitment not to use this information against your partner in future discussions or as ammunition for future fights.

The following exercises are designed to help you and your partner create a safe environment in which to tackle difficult areas of chronic conflict. In such an environment, both partners feel secure enough to reveal what kind of feedback they want, to listen and respond with empathy, and to share feelings—both the good and the bad. Although some

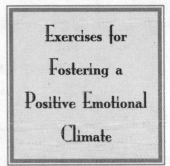

Exercises for Fostering a Positive Emotional Climate

of these exercises may initially strike you as artificial, I suggest you give them all a try.

"MY PERFECT CONVERSATION"

If you often feel frustrated in conversations with your partner, especially about difficult or emotional topics, try "my perfect conversation," an exercise that I created for my clients. In this exercise, the members of the couple take the time, *before* giving the details of their communication, to announce, in general terms, what they want to talk about and what is the ideal response they would like to receive.

Let's have Nancy and Bill serve as our example. They have decided that they will talk about their experiences at work today, and that Nancy will go first. Nancy says to Bill: "I will talk about all the things that went wrong in the day, and some of the good things too. I would like you to look me in the eye as much as you can, smile at me warmly and sympathetically (basically, look friendly and accepting), and say emotionally supportive things like 'That's wonderful, honey,' or 'Oh, I'm so sorry to hear that. . . . That must have been frustrating,' or 'I would have hated that, too.' In short, I want you to put yourself in my place and be as warm and empathetic as possible." Then Nancy talks for five or ten minutes, and Bill tries to do what she asked him to do. Afterward, Nancy gives him positive feedback about what worked well. If Bill does it mostly "wrong" and says nothing but still looks Nancy in the eye and acts warm and accepting, Nancy tells him that she appreciates these positive responses, instead of attacking him for not saying anything. It is extremely important in this exercise to preserve the commitment to stick to positive feedback only.

Now the partners switch roles. Bill says: "I will talk about my day today, and I want you mainly just to listen—without taking what I say and relating it to yourself, or changing the subject, or taking it anywhere else. Even listening silently is fine. I just want to be really heard and accepted fully." Then Nancy listens, and afterward Bill tells her what she did right.

I recommend that you and your partner do this exercise every day or every other day at first. It will take up only ten or twenty minutes of your time, which even the busiest of couples should be able to manage. Eventually, you can practice it from time to time— to keep current on your mutual needs and thus have more satisfying conversations.

THE MIRRORING EXERCISE

Most of us couples therapists have taught clients exercises to help them learn to listen to the messages their partners are sending and play back the spirit and content in a way that captures the essence of the message. The version of the exercise that I have found particularly useful in recent years is one I learned directly from Harville

Hendrix.* To do a version of this exercise, your partner begins by sharing some thoughts and feelings about a subject that upsets him (let's assume he is a man). You listen quietly without interrupting and then try to mirror back what he said. When you are finished, you ask, "Did I mirror you accurately?" (or, "Did I hear you as you wished to be heard?") as well as, "Is there anything else you might be feeling?" Then you listen to your partner's response and mirror that back as accurately and empathetically as you can. After your partner has told you that you heard him well, you tell him, "You make sense," whether you agree with his perceptions fully or not. (I have found that hearing this phrase is especially gratifying for men, who feel very good when their perceptions are validated; women like hearing it, too.) Next, you say to your partner, "I imagine you also might be feeling . . ." and try to put yourself in his shoes, as a sign that you are willing to stretch enough to really imagine what it must feel like to be your mate. Ask your partner again if you mirrored him accurately in your attempt to imagine what he might also be feeling. Then you switch roles, and have your partner mirror your thoughts and feelings about any topic you choose.

THE LOVE LETTER TECHNIQUE

Let's say you are too upset with your partner to want to try to listen with compassion and understanding. You'd rather fire away with blasts of your hurt and anger. If you feel this way, it's time to learn

---

* I learned this version of the exercise from Hendrix directly, at a workshop he gave on couples communication at the Common Boundary Conference in Washington, D.C., in November 1992. Other excellent exercises, including a different version of a mirroring exercise, are found in his book *Getting the Love You Want: A Guide for Couples* (New York: HarperCollins, 1990, paperback edition), pp. 245–73. (The original edition of this book was published in hardcover by Henry Holt and Company in 1988.)

an exercise created by John Gray.* This exercise involves writing a "love letter" to your partner in which you walk through a series of feelings from negative to positive in order to clarify and let go of whatever is blocking you from communicating openly with your partner. To write a love letter to your partner, go off by yourself to collect your thoughts and feelings, and imagine that your partner is listening to this letter with love and understanding. Begin with the anger section; then sadness; then fear; then regret; then love. Include all five sections in every letter, writing a few sentences about each feeling. Try to keep each section about the same length, and write in simple terms. Don't stop until you have expressed your love in the final section. Sign the letter.

Note that in the anger section, you can also express feelings of hurt or frustration. In the sadness section, you can write about feeling disappointed. Include in the regret section apologies, feeling sorry, feeling embarrassed or ashamed, wishing that things had gone differently. The love section is the place for appreciations, positive wishes, and impulses, or just a simple, straightforward expression of your love.

After you have written a love letter, write a response letter to yourself that reflects exactly what you would want your partner to write to you if she or he read your love letter in the most accepting way. Suggested phrases for starting out response letters are: "Thank you for . . ." "I understand . . ." "I am sorry . . ." "You deserve . . ." "I want . . ." "I love you . . ." Often, after completing this process of writing both letters, you will find it is not necessary to share any of this material with your partner. You will be in a more open and loving state and ready to communicate about the subject or task at hand. But you may discover that it works better for you to share these letters. That's fine, too. (You may even feel

---

* John Gray's love letter technique appears in several of his books. I found it in *Men Are from Mars, Women Are from Venus* (New York: HarperCollins, 1992), p. 209.

so complete after writing the initial love letter, you will choose to dispense with writing a perfect response letter, as Dan and Sondra decided to do in chapter 10.) You can use this technique in whichever way suits you best.

POSITIVE WARM-UPS

If you want to keep love and goodwill in your relationship with your partner, it is vital to communicate compliments, appreciations, and other positive strokes. According to Warren Farrell, during the "honeymoon phase" of a relationship the ratio of positive to negative comments tends to be 100 to 1! (That's why it's called the "honeymoon phase." All you can see are the many wonderful traits of your partner.) But after the relationship has been going on for some time, Farrell says that the couple must keep the proportion of positive to negative at 4 to 1 if they are to maintain positive feelings for each other.* As many of us old married couples know, this is easier said than done. We all have a habit of sharing what doesn't work, and of concentrating on the cup being half empty instead of half full. When we reverse this pattern, and work at focusing regularly on what does work, our partner, miraculously, will feel safe enough and appreciated enough to want to change in a more positive direction.

To help you and your mate feel good enough about yourselves and each other to be willing to work toward making some changes for the better, I suggest you begin any communication session by sharing one or two "positive warm-ups" with each other.

---

* I heard Warren Farrell talk on this subject in many presentations about male-female differences over the years. He also writes about it in his book *Why Men Are the Way They Are: The Male-Female Dynamic* (New York: Berkley Books, 1988).

Here are a few opening lines you can choose from to establish an atmosphere of mutual appreciation:

- One of the things I like best about you is . . .
- One of the first things I admired about you was . . .
- I love you most when you . . .
- I like the way you look when you . . .
- We make a good couple because . . .
- I'd like to thank your mother and father for making you . . .
- One of the things I've learned from you is . . .
- One of your strengths that I've benefited from is . . .
- One of the ways you complement (balance) me is . . .
- You make me happy when you . . .
- One of my fondest memories about us is . . .
- One of your most endearing qualities about money is . . .

After each of you has shared one or two warm-ups from the list, you will be in a more positive frame of mind and better able to discuss even thorny issues in your moneylife together.

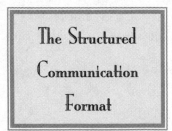

The Structured Communication Format

You are now ready to learn the structured communication technique that I adapted from Isaiah Zimmerman, a clinical psychologist who practices in Washington, D.C. I have been using this technique for about twenty years to help couples communicate clearly and thoroughly—even when discussing the most emotionally charged issues.

To ensure success, agree to abide by the following ground rules:

* *Set an approximate time limit for each communication.* Limit your sharing to no longer than three minutes or so, to avoid long monologues or tirades.

* *Observe the no-interruption rule.* Do not interrupt when your partner has the floor, and try to listen undefensively and with an open mind as much as possible.

* *Announce the nature of the message you will be sending.* Select from four main channels of communication: (1) the "upset" channel; (2) thoughts and feelings when you are not upset; (3) the empathetic listening channel; and (4) the negotiation channel.

   If you are feeling angry, hurt, resentful, disappointed—stirred up in any way—say, "I'm angry," or "I'm hurt," or "I'm upset." If you want to share a neutral or positive thought or feeling, tell your partner, "I have a thought (or a feeling) I want to share." To see if you understand your partner's point of view, announce, "I want to verify how you feel about this." And finally, if you want to negotiate about something, say, "I have a negotiation." In any of these cases, identifying and announcing the nature of the message will make your partner feel respected and "warned" about where you want to go in your communication.

* *Ask whether your partner is willing to listen.* Give your partner some time to consider, "Can I truly listen with an open mind, or do I already have a defensive response to what I imagine you might say?"

* *Respect a no as well as a yes.* Communicate only when and if your partner is willing to listen. If the answer is yes, your partner should say yes; if not, he or she should have full permission to say no—for now.

* *If you say no to listening, take the initiative in continuing the dialogue.* The one who says no can either ask for time to share upset or

negative feelings that are blocking the listening process, or ask to return to this discussion at a specific time in the future.

* *If you say yes, commit to listening undefensively and without interrupting.*

* *Announce when you're finished.*

* *Verify your partner's feelings whenever possible.* If your partner has shared a feeling, and you are willing to verify or mirror what was said and felt, then do so. Next ask, "Did I hear you as you wished to be heard?" (You don't say, "Did I get it right?" because one of the most important reasons for playing back or verifying what you heard is to communicate the spirit of the content as well as its literal meaning.) After that, your partner can give you feedback on whether you gave an appropriate response, missed something, or misheard something.

* *Verification does not have to be followed by feedback.* If your partner has verified your message poorly, and you find yourself angry that he or she *didn't* hear you in the right spirit, beware of lunging into a full-scale attack about how often you are unheard and misunderstood. If you need to share your anger, it is fine to announce that you have an upset feeling, ask if your partner is willing to listen, and communicate your anger or disappointment at being misunderstood. Or, if you feel grateful for your partner's attempt to understand, you could share a positive feeling (with permission, of course), before deciding to give your partner feedback on whether he or she heard you as you wished to be heard.

* *Don't negotiate before feelings are aired.* Share negative feelings with your partner, and have your partner listen and verify your feelings with empathy and compassion. Difficult feelings must be aired, shared, and understood before a couple can negotiate successfully.

* *Negotiation is the only action channel.* If you do want to negotiate some changes in action or behavior, first offer something your partner might want, and then ask for what you want. This is a polite protocol but is not absolutely necessary. The only things that can be negotiated are actions and behaviors. Feelings *cannot* be negotiated. So while you can ask your mate not to yell at you, you can't ask your mate not to be angry. We all have the right to feel whatever emotions have a grip on us.

* *Try sitting back-to-back.* Sometimes one partner or both feel safer and can open up more if they don't make eye contact while sharing difficult material. I recommend that you and your partner share hurt, angry, or stirred-up feelings while sitting back-to-back, and turn to face each other when you exchange neutral or positive remarks.

* *Here are some options if tempers flare.* Consider taking a break until you can look at what got you so riled up with a little more objectivity. Another alternative is to try sitting back-to-back and asking for permission to communicate in the "upset" mode. Once you have gotten a genuine yes, you can push out your upset feeling until you really feel a sense of closure (until you're thinking: "Whew! I'm glad I said this. It felt so good to get it out. What a relief!").

Now that you know the framework of this structured communication format, here is the order in which I recommend that you practice it.

1. Establish a safe climate with positive warm-ups. (See preceding section for examples.)

2. Share hurt, angry, resentful, stirred-up feelings. (Consider sitting back-to-back, at least for this part, and perhaps until the last step.)

3. Listen empathetically and verify each other's feelings wherever possible, before moving on to your own emotional reactions. If you can't, share your own upsets first, and verify or mirror later.

4. Negotiate with each other, and suggest actions and behaviors that would alter your usual patterns.

5. Share positive cool-downs such as the following:
   * What I most appreciated about you today was . . .
   * When you express yourself, I value the way you . . .
   * Here's what I appreciated about what you said . . .
   * I learned to understand you better by . . .
   * You helped me feel understood and heard when you . . .

If you have practiced any of these techniques in the course of reading this chapter, I suggest that you reward yourself for this new behavior, and monitor your thoughts and feelings about what it was like to do them.

Using These Techniques in Structured Moneytalks

Having learned a variety of couples communication techniques, you are now ready to begin exploring together in more depth each of your histories around money. In the first structured moneytalk (chapter 9), where I give you the subjects to discuss and the order in which to discuss them, you need only use a few aspects of the structured communication format. You don't have to sit back-to-back, or ask for permission to communicate in prescribed channels. But I do recommend that you listen respectfully and observe the no-interruption rule, make a commitment not to use any of this shared information against your partner at a later date, and start with warm-ups and end with cool-downs. Toward the end of the session, you may also want to verify and mirror what your partner has shared. When you move on to more loaded topics in the second structured moneytalk (chapter 10), you need to observe the full set of guidelines presented in this chapter.

9

Structured Moneytalk 1: Sharing

Your Money History

Remember Devon and Karen from chapter 7? Devon was a money monk who cherished his simple lifestyle. He felt comfortable making only $25,000 a year in Washington, D.C., an expensive city to live in, where he worked for a nonprofit environmental firm. He had great contempt for the "bourgeois" people around him who drove expensive cars and went on elaborate vacations in fancy places. His own car was an old Volkswagen Beetle that was falling apart. Karen, his wife, was a money amasser—at least, compared with Devon. A lawyer for an activist firm, she was contemplating buying herself a Honda Accord and hoping to take a nice summer vacation with her husband. But her money monk spouse scoffed at such ideas. As the first step in a communication process that could bring them closer to each other, Devon and Karen decided to have a moneytalk to share their money history. Karen remarked, and Devon agreed, that though they had been together for more than five years and shared a lot in other areas,

they really didn't know much about each other's past when it came
to money.

In this chapter, we will listen in on Devon and Karen's moneytalk. I will also give you an outline so you and your partner can
have a similar conversation of your own. If you are in a committed
relationship, whether the two of you are a new couple, or have been
together for a long, long time, I'll bet that, like Devon and Karen,
you still don't know a lot about each other's money history. Since
money has been such a taboo subject in our culture, sharing details
on past experiences with money is not usually done in the course of
normal communication. But if you both take the time to do this
now, bearing in mind all you've just learned about respectful communication, you will be pleasantly surprised at how much closer
you feel to each other. Note that this first structured moneytalk
is for sharing information and feelings, not for exploring conflicts
between you in the area of money. Here are general suggestions to
follow as you proceed:

* *Find an unstressful time to have this talk.* Set aside time when
neither of you is hassled or stressed, and when your attention is not
divided. In this way, you both can devote quality time to this initial
sharing session and listen to each other with as much patience and
respect as possible.

* *Begin with warm-ups.* Choose one or two of my warm-up messages (see pp. 169–70), or create your own, to communicate what
you appreciate about your partner or about your couple connection.

* *Share each response in turn, and do not interrupt the speaker.*
The listener's task is merely to listen respectfully and with empathy.

* *Use your most effective communication style.* You may decide to
write down all your responses first, separately, and then share them

with each other after you finish reading this chapter; or you can write down one response at a time and then share the results right away. If you function best spontaneously, it is perfectly all right to respond verbally, trusting that what emerges is what you want and need to say. Don't worry if you and your partner have different preferences; one of you could, for example, write down the responses, and the other could simply share them verbally. Finally, you have the option of sticking closely to the outline I provide, or changing the order around a bit.

✹ *Skip over—for the time being—any material you cannot answer.* But I recommend that you think about it later. Try to come back at another time and share with your partner the answers you come up with.

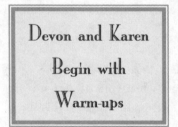

Devon and Karen Begin with Warm-ups

KAREN: I appreciate the way you've been fixing me dinner the nights I have to work late at my law office, and how you haven't gotten grouchy or complained about my crazy late schedule. I know it's lonely for you to be alone at night so often, and I really appreciate how you haven't taken your feelings out on me one little bit.

DEVON: I appreciate your sense of humor in general. When I get too intense and serious about my environmental work, you have a way of lightening me up that doesn't make me feel criticized or put down.

As a result of sharing their positive appreciations, Devon and Karen already felt much closer, and more willing to open up to each other.

Here are the points to address in the first stretch of sharing. (For a discussion of the messages about money that we receive during our childhood, refer back to chapter 2.)

> ## Sharing Your Money History: Beginning with Your Childhood

* This is how my parents handled money:
    * how they spent it . . .
    * how they saved it . . .
    * how they talked about it (or didn't talk about it, or screamed about it, or worried aloud about it) . . .
    * how they dealt with allowances with me (and my siblings) . . .

* Here are some of my specific childhood money memories:
    * of my parents . . .
    * of siblings and other relatives . . .
    * of my peers . . .
    * of school (with teachers or mentors of any kind) . . .
    * of religious school (if this applies) . . .

* From my family, I received (either directly or indirectly) the money messages that . . .

* From my peers, I received (either directly or indirectly) the money messages that . . .

* From my religious training, I received the money messages that . . .

* From the culture at large (from books, TV, advertisements, movies, etc.), I received the money messages that . . .

* Here's how I reacted to these messages . . .

* I made the following vows about my moneylife:
    * to be just like _____ in this way . . .
    * *never* to be like _____ in this way . . .

    ✴   to deal with money in this way . . .
    ✴   and to . . .

  ✴ In my family, I think that money symbolized (*choices:* love, power, control, independence, dependency, self-worth, security, freedom, corruption, and/or any other responses that seem to fit) . . .

Remember that both of you can share all your responses at once or divide them up into several chunks. Another option is to have one of you share all your answers right away and the other deliver them piecemeal. It is important to respect your partner's capacity to give and receive information in manageable parcels. That way, neither member feels overloaded or stressed and doesn't risk becoming irritable or defensive.

    After you and your partner have finished communicating this information, decide if you need to take a break or if you both are ready and willing to go on to the next section, in which you will explore how the past may be impinging on the present.

Devon and Karen's First Sharing of Past History

Devon had read my outline and jotted down notes on each point, which he referred to as he told Karen about his money history.

DEVON: My father was a bricklayer who worked day and night to make enough money to survive. My mom stayed home with us eight kids and slaved around the house all day, trying to keep our home manageable. They never fought about money. Mom was frugal, and they both knew they didn't have a lot. We rarely went on a vacation. How did my family spend money? Only on necessities. How did they save it? They had virtually nothing to save. How did they talk about it? They both criticized the rich, greedy people who had money but did nothing with it except to enhance themselves selfishly. My dad sometimes worked for those filthy rich people—that's what he called them, in fact—and he would talk about the disgusting amount of waste he saw in their homes.

As far as allowances are concerned, we never got any, until each kid was about fifteen. Then I got $5 a week, and I had to pay for my pleasures out of that. We all wore hand-me-down clothes. Sometimes we kids fought with one another about wanting what the other had, but that seemed normal in our big family. Our big treat was going to a movie about once a month. Once my father caught my brother Lou stealing candy in a store. Dad beat him and didn't let him watch TV or leave the house for a week, except to go to school.

We went to Catholic school, where many of the kids were pretty poor, but there were others who had much more money than we did. We felt superior to the rich kids, in a strange way: We thought we were purer than they were and knew about "real life" in the "real world." We actually talked about how we would go to heaven, and the rich kids would probably go to hell! The nuns said things like "Money is the root of all evil," and I believed them completely. And I guess I still do! In some way, money symbolizes to me greed and corruption. I guess I fit the money monk description perfectly, don't I? [Karen took care not to respond to this question by saying, "You sure do, and it drives me nuts sometimes!" She just listened respectfully.]

When I think about my childhood and the money messages I got from that time, I think I told myself not to focus on any of the material deprivation I may have felt. I told myself I would make sure that money was just never that important to me; and that I would never become greedy, selfish, and corrupt, like those guys my dad worked for in those big brick houses.

Now it was Karen's turn to share. She had decided to do this spontaneously, without writing down her answers first. But she had read the statements in advance and had thought about what she remembered from her childhood.

KAREN: I grew up in a wealthy suburb of Chicago. We had everything we wanted, pretty much. My parents were different from each other. My mom liked to spend money on beautiful things for the house, and lovely clothes for her and the kids, and for my father, too. My dad preferred to save his money for great vacations, and for the future (to save for college for us kids, and for retirement). My folks argued about how to spend or save, but the arguments weren't too terrible: like low-level static in our home.

My brothers were older than I was, and got more money for their allowance, of course. I thought that was unfair, and I told my folks, but they just smiled and patted me on the head.

Most of my friends at school had a fair amount of money, too. But there was one girl in my class, Bobbie, my good friend, who came from a much poorer family. I used to lend her money for lunch a lot, and for clothes sometimes, too. My parents found out about it and told me not to do that anymore. I think I felt guilty about having more money than Bobbie. But I also liked being able to help her out. I was afraid to cross my parents and stopped lending her money. But I was too ashamed to tell her why. This created a big rift in our relationship. For weeks, she barely talked to me. I was hurt about the tension and distance I felt between us. I think I vowed that when I was older, I would try to make a lot of money and help a lot of people who didn't have as much as I did. I think that fuels my desire to make more money today: both to enjoy it myself and to give some of it away. To me, money symbolizes freedom and independence. The more I have of it, the more I can do what I really want—at least, that's what I tell myself.

Karen felt she had shared enough for now. She and Devon agreed to return to their moneytalk the next afternoon, when she could share more of her money history, and listen to the next piece of Devon's. This amount of sharing had already made them more sensitive to each other's feelings. Devon started to understand why Karen wanted to buy herself a Honda Accord, for example, and Karen began mentally scaling down her vacation plans, so that Devon would be more comfortable going along with her. And Devon's realization that his family had hardly ever taken a vacation helped him be more open to expanding his ability to tolerate pleasure in this area.

If you and your partner are ready and willing to listen, go on and share this information with each other:

> **Back to You: Getting to Know You Better**

* Today, I think that money symbolizes (*choices:* happiness, love, power, control, independence, dependency, self-worth, security, freedom, corruption, and/or any other responses that seem to fit) . . .

* Here's how I handled money before we met . . .

* I am closest to the following money personality types (*choices:* hoarder, spender, binger, money monk, money avoider, money worrier, money amasser, risk taker, and/or risk avoider) . . .

* I would like to move toward this money type (or types) . . .

* I would like to move away from this money type (or types) . . .

* Here are some other ways that I'd like to change my money attitudes and behaviors . . .

* You might be able to help me move closer to my goals by . . .

N.B.: The last sentence is tricky to complete. Avoid saying to your partner things like, "If you would spend less, I could spend more." Instead, consider asking for help with your own issues only if you are truly willing to take help from your partner in this area. If not, you may want to skip this sentence and possibly return to it at a later time.

Karen and Devon
Continue Their
Moneytalk

To discuss the points in the preceding section, Karen and Devon decided to go back and forth, sharing information in smaller chunks. This time, Karen went first.

KAREN: I think money still symbolizes freedom and independence to me. It also symbolizes power somewhat: both power to have and do what you want, and power in the world, both for good and for evil.

Before we met, I used to indulge myself more: eating out in fancy restaurants when I had the money—and feeling somewhat guilty about this, since some of my friends couldn't afford to eat out. I used to buy more clothes than I needed and plan more and more lavish vacations. I guess I am a combination spender and money amasser, a little bit of a worrier, with little flickers of money monk consciousness thrown in. I'm a little afraid of being too wealthy and losing my values, but I really don't think I will. When it comes to investing, though I haven't had much to invest, I'm a risk avoider.

DEVON: I think money still symbolizes greed and corruption to me. I still pride myself on my simple lifestyle. I like driving around in my old VW bug, and I like the fact that we have only one car and ride our bikes and take public transportation a lot, even though it takes us more time to get to work. I am clearly a money monk and, to some extent, a money avoider. I just don't like to deal with the details of my moneylife at all. I'm happy to have you take care of all of that for both of us! I'm glad I make only $25,000 a year; that seems like more than enough, even in Washington, D.C. Most people in this town think that that's barely enough to survive on, but it only makes me feel more proud and defiant!

KAREN: I'd like to worry less about money and be less obsessed with making sure I have enough to be able to do anything I want to do. I'd also like to feel fine about spending it on my own pleasure, as long as I do it in moderation, and still give away some money to causes I want to support. I'd like to decrease the tension between us when it comes to buying a car, taking a vacation, et cetera. You could help me by agreeing not to *act* judgmental when I do want to give myself pleasure—even if you *feel* judgmental sometimes. You could also help me see that I am free to pursue my dreams and goals, even if I don't have a tremendous amount of money. You could do this by listening to me talk about my deeper longings and goals and dreams in life, and brainstorming with me about how I could achieve them.

DEVON: I'd like to be less rigid in my avoidance of money matters and less contemptuous toward others about money. It's hard for me to admit this, but I actually would like to trust myself more and know that more money will not make me sell out and lose my commitment to the values I hold dear. I *would* like to enjoy nice vacations with you without feeling guilty; and maybe my old car *is* falling apart, and I could tolerate it if you did buy a Honda Accord and if we used it sometimes to go to work. God! I'm actually flinching while I say this; but I know rationally that what you want is not awful or ridiculous but is really okay—for you, at least! And maybe, eventually, even for me! You could help me with all this by agreeing not to act judgmental about my extreme money monk tendencies but to slowly and gently help me to stretch a little beyond them. And maybe if we balanced our checkbooks together, at the same time, I wouldn't hate keeping track of my money so much.

Preserving Safety in Your Own Structured Moneytalk

Once you have shared with your partner this information about yourself, remember to respect the fragile nature of this communication. Take care not to use any of this information against your partner, now or in the future. It is always tempting to say, "I always knew your tightness came from your lousy father!" Or, "Well, now that you know that about yourself, what are you gonna do about it?" If you want this process to deepen your relationship and your intimacy, it is crucial that you create a safe space in which information can be shared and heard.

Optional Portions of the Moneytalk

SECOND MARRIAGES

If you have been married before, or lived with a partner in an intimate relationship for quite some time, it may be useful to share the following information with your new partner. Remember, each of you takes a turn, with no interruptions, comments, judgments, or even questions from the listener.

- In my last significant relationship (marriage), we handled money as follows . . .
- We used to fight about . . .
- After that experience, I vowed that never again would I . . .
- Some of the things I learned and value from that experience are . . .

When you share these statements, avoid getting into heated discussions about any loaded issues. You can save that for the second structured moneytalk in the next chapter.

SHARING YOUR MONEY DIALOGUES

If both of you have written money dialogues (see chapter 5), and if you are both willing, share them with each other to conclude this communication process. If you are the only one who has done a dialogue, do not share it with your partner; you might end up feeling too vulnerable. Take care not to attack your mate for not having done the dialogue. Focus instead on the progress you have made in this moneytalk and the positive sharing that was accomplished.

MIRRORING WHAT YOUR PARTNER SHARED

This sharing process may bring up fairly loaded issues. As noted, do *not* plunge into them right now. Instead, practice the mirroring (hearing and listening) exercise described in chapter 8, to put yourself in your partner's shoes and try to empathize with his or her feelings.

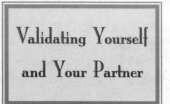

Here is the final series of sentences for you to complete:

- Here's what I appreciate about the work I've done today . . .
- Here's what I appreciate about the work you have done today with me . . .
- Some of the important things I remembered (or shared) about myself were . . .
- I am glad that you told me . . .
- To reward ourselves for having had this moneytalk, I suggest we both . . .

N.B.: A joint reward is preferable, but two separate rewards are all right, too. If you're feeling particularly celebratory, you could even decide to give yourselves both a joint reward and individual ones.

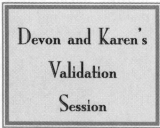

Devon and Karen had accomplished a tremendous amount in this open and honest moneytalk. Here's what they appreciated about themselves and each other:

DEVON: I appreciated that I was willing to focus on subjects related to money for such a long time—for me!—and to take the time and make the effort to complete all the statements in the outline. Also, that I was willing to admit some of my own shortcomings and rigidities around my money monk personality.

I appreciated your openness in sharing similar information about yourself. I never felt judged or attacked by you; and I *really* appreciated that! I learned about ways that your childhood was totally different from mine, and ways that you were hurt by not being able to be as generous as you wanted to be. That made me feel much closer to you. I'd like to reward ourselves by having a picnic in the park and maybe even going to a movie later! [Devon laughed at his tentativeness about spending money on his own pleasure. He had become much more aware of his knee-jerk guilt reaction to "selfish" spending on personal pleasure.]

KAREN: I appreciated my own willingness to look at my imperfections and warts around money. I also appreciated my commitment to remain gentle and nonjudgmental with you, and to listen carefully and respectfully. It's a habit I'd like to practice more and more.

I appreciated your honesty with me about areas of your life around money you didn't feel great about. I learned a lot from hearing about your Catholic school training. What you told me about your dad and mom judging wealthy people really helps me understand you better. I think I'll be able to be more tolerant of, and gentle with, the money monk in you. And now I can see that the money monk in me needs to do a little work, too! I think your reward of a picnic in the park *and* a movie later is a great idea. I accept.

Do not be concerned if you feel you did not accomplish as much as Karen and Devon did in your own first structured moneytalk. At the very least, you opened up a channel of communication that will eventually lead to better sharing and deeper intimacy—especially if you keep practicing good communication skills.

If you are both not feeling overloaded, set a date for your next moneytalk, in which you will both confront and resolve more emotionally loaded topics or more highly charged dynamics in your couple relationship. (See chapter 10.) If you are not yet ready to commit to a specific date, agree to return within a certain period of time (in the next two weeks, for example, or before a month is out). This will help you sustain the forward movement of the process.

10.

Structured Moneytalk 2:

Tackling Your Money Conflicts

Now that you and your partner have spent some time talking about the emotional loads from the past that have impinged on your respective relationships with money today, you are ready to embark on a more dangerous exploration: discussing areas of conflict in your moneylife together. If you use the techniques of structured communication that I taught you in chapter 8, you should be able to navigate successfully through these deep and sometimes choppy waters.

Since this process is one of the more difficult legs of your journey toward money harmony, I have provided a sample conversation so you can see exactly how one couple conducted this type of moneytalk. I strongly recommend that you read this conversation carefully before attempting your own moneytalk with your partner.

The couple I have selected are Dan and Sondra, whom we met in chapter 7.

As you may remember, Dan was a hoarder and a worrier; Sondra was a spender and a money avoider. For Dan, money equaled security; for Sondra, money equaled love. They had been a couple ever since high school, and had recently had a painful fight about their fifteenth anniversary. Dan had spent hours and hours in record stores looking for "their song"—"My Prayer"—which he thought would make a very thoughtful and sentimental anniversary present. When he found it, he was ecstatic. But Sondra was very hurt when she saw the gift: the record seemed chintzy and insignificant to her. She had been hoping for an expensive piece of jewelry. After Sondra told him what she thought of his gift, Dan also felt hurt and misunderstood. These recent hard feelings were clouding their other interactions. And now they were about to take a one-week vacation together without their two kids. They both had fears about how this supposedly romantic vacation would go. In the midst of all this, Dan and Sondra decided to try to have a structured moneytalk about the vacation and their disparate money styles.

Dan and Sondra Prepare for the Moneytalk

WRITING "LOVE LETTERS"

Dan and Sondra agreed to devote a half hour to writing "love letters" to each other in private. The subject of the letters was to be the bad feelings after the anniversary gift incident. (For more information on this technique, refer back to chapter 8.) Dan's love letter to Sondra is as follows:

Dear Sondra:

I feel upset that you didn't like my anniversary gift of "My Prayer," our old song. I am frustrated that I looked for hours and hours in record stores for a sentimental and romantic gift I thought would please you, and it didn't work.

I am disappointed that you didn't appreciate this gift and the love and effort that went into it.

I worry that whatever I do give you, it'll never be enough, or never be the right thing.

I feel bad about hurting your feelings in my choice of a gift. That was the last thing in the world I wanted to do. I know you tend to feel unloved if gifts aren't worth a lot of money, and maybe I should have remembered that in choosing this gift. I'm sorry I didn't—for both of us.

I love the times when you give me gifts that are simple and from the heart: like the poem you wrote me for our last anniversary. I appreciate all the ways you support me in my life. I love you and want to make you happy.

Love, Dan

After writing this letter, Dan felt less hurt and angry, and much more aware of the things he did get from his relationship with his wife.

Here is Sondra's love letter to Dan:

Dear Dan:

I am angry that you bought me such a chintzy little gift for our anniversary. It made me feel like I wasn't worth very much to you.

I am sad that we had hurt and tension around the giving of these gifts, and that these bad feelings almost spoiled our night out together to celebrate our anniversary. I wish we could have resolved our differences more lovingly.

I am afraid that we are so different that neither of us will ever get our real needs met by the other. I don't want us to drift apart—I want us to find a way to get closer.

I am sorry I reacted so strongly to the old record you bought. When I remember that money doesn't equal love, I can appreciate the sentimental and romantic nature of your gift, and the time and effort you took to get it for me.

I know you try hard to please me in a lot of ways. I'm sorry I don't tell you more often about the ways I do appreciate you. I'm sorry I tend to be so critical and attacking when I feel hurt and rejected.

I love you and will try to do better. I will try to understand that you have a different style of gift giving than I do, and not take it to mean that you don't care. I know you do, and I do, too.

Love, Sondra

In writing her love letter, Sondra was able to let go of a large chunk of her anger and hurt, and begin to appreciate the effort Dan had made, in his way, to please her.

Both Dan and Sondra thought about writing "response letters" to themselves. (Remember, with a response letter you write your reaction to the love letter you have just composed, pretending to be your partner and responding with the exact words you want to hear.) But they felt so much better after writing the love letters that they decided they could dispense with the responses. They also saw no need to share their love letters with each other.

Having gotten out their feelings about their anniversary, Don and Sondra were now able to move toward their moneytalk with less emotional baggage.

PRACTICING "MY PERFECT CONVERSATION"

Dan was generally a "thinking type" in his communication style, tending to talk logically and give advice in conversation. Sondra

was a "feeling type," who tended to share feelings in a fairly emotional way. Because their styles were so different, they decided that
doing the "perfect conversation" exercise (see chapter 8) would be
useful preparation for their moneytalk. The topic for sharing would
be stresses at work. Sondra, a schoolteacher, went first. She asked
that Dan respond with empathetic comments such as "That must
be hard" and positive comments like "You're very good at that"
while looking her in the eye.

SONDRA: The kids at school are driving me crazy lately, and my
    principal is absolutely no help!
DAN: It must be frustrating work in that kind of stressful environ-
    ment, with so little support from your boss. . . . I'd hate to have
    to deal with kids like that!
SONDRA: It is . . . but at least with Freddy, my most difficult kid, I
    see some slow signs of progress. He didn't even have one tantrum
    today!
DAN: You're a great teacher, I know. I'd love to see you in action
    with him!

After this short interchange, Sondra told him what he did *right*.

SONDRA: You looked me in the eye, and responded to me sensitively
    when you said, "You're a great teacher" and "I'd hate to have to
    deal with kids like that."

Now it was Dan's turn. He wanted Sondra mainly to listen and
not to make too many suggestions about what he might do differently. But he indicated he would appreciate some degree of intellec-
tual response to the situation. This is what he said about his work
stresses as a corporate executive.

DAN: My job is driving me crazy, too. This guy who works under me is so difficult; he refuses to do what I tell him to do; I feel like he's trying to undermine me . . . and if he keeps this up, we'll never meet our deadline this month! I'm tempted to just fire the bastard, I'm so frustrated!

SONDRA: I know you're trying your hardest, and this is such a difficult situation in itself.

DAN: You can't imagine how hard I work to try to get projects finished on time! But this guy is so slow; he just keeps dragging his feet!

SONDRA: You know, I've been reading about how to resolve conflict with workers by trying to look at what would be a win-win solution for both parties. Maybe if you identify the goal you both want and need, you could figure out a new way to approach this difficult guy.

Sondra curtailed her tendency to preach at Dan. (She was prone to say things like, "When I'm in that situation, here's what I do . . ." or, "You need to be more patient with . . .") Dan went on to give her positive feedback only.

DAN: In general, you listened well, and I felt supported by you. You didn't preach at me or tell me what I'm doing wrong. I appreciated that. I especially liked it when you told me about ideas in the field of conflict resolution about win-win solutions. That was interesting.

In this positive frame of mind, Dan and Sondra were ready to progress to the more loaded topic at hand.

AGREEING ON TOPICS TO DISCUSS

Dan wanted to discuss Sondra's tendency to overspend and not keep track of the money, and his fears that she would act this way on vacation. Sondra wanted to talk about Dan's tightness and money worry, and the possibility that these traits would prevent them from enjoying their vacation. They agreed to talk about both topics under the subject of "fears and hopes about our vacation."

AGREEING ON GROUND RULES

To make this potentially difficult moneytalk as safe as possible, Dan and Sondra agreed to the following:

- We will not interrupt each other.
- We'll start this moneytalk sitting back-to-back, so we each can stay more closely in touch with our feelings; and we'll turn around later, when either of us feels the need for more eye contact. We'll definitely talk face-to-face during the positive cooldown toward the end of the moneytalk.
- We will announce in advance the nature of our communications, and ask whether the other person is willing to listen.
- We will attempt to avoid long, punitive tirades, limiting each communication to about three minutes.
- We will say "I'm finished" when we each of us feels we have completed our communication.
- We will start with positive warm-ups.

- Next, we will share grudges, hurts, and resentments, in order to try to get rid of them quickly and efficiently.
- After one person shares a difficult or emotional message, the other will try to mirror it back before responding to it with equal emotional charge.
- Finally, we'll try to negotiate about what we both want on this vacation.
- We'll agree to end the moneytalk by sharing cool-downs: positive appreciations of each other.
- We'll try to set a time to have the next moneytalk.

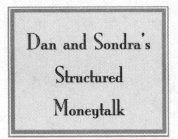

Dan and Sondra's Structured Moneytalk

EXCHANGING POSITIVE WARM-UPS

DAN: I appreciate your ability to enjoy life, and to make our home a beautiful place for our family. I also appreciate your planning fun things for our family to do.

SONDRA: I appreciate how hard you work to support us, how you do our taxes and pay bills on time, and keep our life organized around money. I also appreciate what a good father you are to the kids.

Anchored in their good feelings, Dan and Sondra were willing to take the plunge into rockier areas. Still, their defenses had to be addressed early on.

SHARING OLD HURTS, RESENTMENTS, AND FEARS

SONDRA: Dan, I feel upset about something. Are you willing to listen?

DAN (feeling defensive already): No. I feel defensive and need to share my fear. Are you willing to listen?

Sondra understood that Dan needed to clear the decks in his mind, so to speak, to be able to hear her. Therefore, she responded:

SONDRA: Yes. I'm willing to listen.

DAN: I bet you're going to attack me for my stinginess, and I'm sick of hearing about that. Talk about something different for a change! I'm finished!

Having got that defensive response off his chest, Dan was willing to listen to Sondra:

SONDRA: I yearn to be able to discuss spending and saving, avoiding and worrying about money in a new, nonadversarial way. I'm willing to spend time getting out some old resentments, but I want to move past them quickly, and not get stuck in the old, awful, negative places. I hope you want that too. I'm finished.

DAN: I want to mirror back what you just said. Are you willing to listen?

SONDRA (happy about that): Yes!

DAN: You hope we can have a friendlier discussion about our differences than the blaming fights we usually have. Did I hear you as you wished to be heard?

SONDRA: Yes, you did. I'm finished.

I can't stress enough the importance of verifying feelings in this way.

DAN: I'm worried about something. Are you willing to listen?

SONDRA: Yes.

DAN: Sondra, I'm sick of living in fear and dread of what you're
gonna spend money on next. I'm sick of doing all the worrying
in this family about whether we have enough for this vacation,
this new piece of furniture, this new purchase for the kids. You
didn't grow up with a father who lost everything in the Depression, so you have no idea how that feels. Living with your overspending keeps me in a constant state of anxiety. I hate it, and I
want it to stop! I'm finished.

Pushing out his feelings like this was new for Dan, who usually
stopped short of fully expressing himself. This response enabled
him to break through to a new place, and he started crying softly,
feeling how painful this conflict was in his life. His vulnerability
melted Sondra's defenses, and she was able to verify his feelings
without going into her own anger in defense or response.

SONDRA: I want to see if I heard you right. Are you willing to listen?
DAN: Yes.
SONDRA: You feel tremendously burdened by worries over money,
and my unconscious way of spending too much money all the
time drives you crazy. You're tired of doing all the worrying for
the whole family, and you want me to stop overspending. Did I
hear you as you wished to be heard?

Dan felt moved by how well Sondra had heard his feelings.

DAN: I have feedback for you. Are you willing to listen?
SONDRA: Sure.
DAN: You got it exactly. I'm finished.
DAN: I have a positive feeling to share. Are you willing to listen?
SONDRA: Yes.

DAN: I can't tell you how good it feels to me that you heard me so well, so simply and clearly. Thank you so much. I'm finished.

Dan still felt stirred up, so he went on to vent his feeling:

DAN: I have another stirred-up feeling. Are you willing to listen?
SONDRA: Yes.
DAN: I'm so exhausted from overworking, worrying, and feeling so alone in my concerns that the family will always have enough. I wish you could share this burden with me more fully, without getting more exhausted yourself. I'm finished.

It was time for Sondra to take some time and space for her own old feelings.

SONDRA: I'm upset about something. Are you willing to listen?
DAN: Yes.
SONDRA: I hate it that you worry and overwork so much. I wish you'd spend more time with me and the kids. If you would, I might not use all my free time to run around in stores and shop. I think a part of your worry is exaggerated and a result of your terrible fearful childhood.

Now I have an attack on myself: "Sondra, you *do* need to get more conscious of your spending and stop spending to get back at Dan for not being around. It's a lousy way to conduct your life! Grow up and start asking Dan for what you really want: more time alone with him!"

And you, Dan, need to listen to my good advice about working less. If you worked less, I'd spend less, and we'd both have more love in our life together. And if you won't consider this, I probably will go on overspending and driving you nuts about this forever. It's time you took my advice in an area where I *do* have some expertise: knowing how to create quality family time! I'm finished.

Now it was Dan's turn to be generous.

DAN: I want to verify what you said. Are you willing to listen?

SONDRA: Yes.

DAN: You feel that I worry and overwork too much, partly because of my difficult, fearful childhood. You want me to consider working less and spending more quality time at home, with you and the kids, and with you alone. If I do that, you would spend less money. Did I hear you as you wished to be heard?

SONDRA: I have feedback. Wanna hear it?

DAN: Sure.

SONDRA: You heard me just fine. I'm finished.

Just from hearing each other's irrational frustrations, and mirroring them back, they felt much more hopeful about addressing present concerns about their upcoming vacation.

MOVING ON TO THE PRESENT

SONDRA: Dan, I have a concern I want to share. Are you willing to listen?

DAN: Okay.

SONDRA: I don't want to spend every minute of this vacation looking over my shoulder to see you breathing down my neck about how much money to spend on special things for myself and gifts for the kids. I want you to lighten up about this, and trust me that I won't be totally unreasonable when it comes to buying souvenirs. I'm finished.

DAN: I have a concern. Are you willing to listen?

SONDRA: Okay.

DAN: I don't want to worry that all you want to do on vacation is buy more things we don't need. If you would agree to set limits on yourself, and to tell me what those limits are, maybe I could agree to work on letting go of my money anxiety—at least during this vacation! But I'm afraid that with you, especially on vacation, the sky's the limit! I'm finished.

Now each was willing to verify the other's upset feelings.

SONDRA: I want to mirror back what you said. Are you willing to listen?

DAN: Yes.

SONDRA: You're afraid that unless I agree to set a ceiling on my own vacation spending, I'll really go wild and spend all our money, sending you into a massive case of anxiety and worry about our money. You want me to set reasonable limits on this vacation, and tell you what they are, so you can relax. Did I hear you as you wished to be heard?

DAN (pleased that Sondra heard him well): Yes, you did. I'm finished.

Once you are comfortable with this process, you can experiment with letting go of the requirement that you ask for permission to give feedback. It is vital that you continue to ask for permission and announce the nature of your communication when you are sharing stirred-up feelings of any kind (hurt, anger, fear, etc.).

Dan went on to mirror Sondra's feelings:

DAN: You feel afraid that I'm gonna breathe down your neck about spending money on this vacation, and you want me to trust you more and lay off. You enjoy buying souvenirs of places we've been for you and the kids, and whether I understand that or not, you want me to accept this need of yours and trust that you won't go wild. Did I hear you as you wish to be heard?

SONDRA: Yes. I'm finished.

Both Dan and Sondra now felt that they were ready to try to negotiate about ways to deal with spending on their vacation.

NEGOTIATING WITH EACH OTHER

SONDRA: Dan, I have a negotiation. Are you willing to listen?

DAN: Yes.

SONDRA: I offer to spend only $100 of your money, and up to $100 of my own money, on gifts during this vacation. I want you to refrain from saying nasty things to me about what I buy or acting grouchy in any way about my souvenir shopping. I want you to look pleasant about this, even if you are still feeling somewhat anxious. I'm finished.

DAN: I have a negotiation. Are you willing to listen?

SONDRA: Yes.

DAN: I offer to act pleasant, upbeat, and nonjudgmental about your shopping on vacation. I would like you to spend only $75 of my money, and the rest of your own. I would prefer it if you spent only $75 of your own money, but that's up to you. I'm finished.

SONDRA: I have a little angry feeling. Are you willing to listen?

DAN: Okay.

SONDRA: I feel like a bad kid when you try to tell me how much to spend. I hate it! I also have an attack on myself: "Sondra, if you would ever set real limits on yourself, your husband wouldn't have to set them for you! Grow up!" I'm finished.

Now that Sondra had expressed these sentiments, she could return to negotiation:

SONDRA: Dan, I have a negotiation. Are you willing to listen?
DAN: Yes.
SONDRA: I accept your negotiation. I'm finished.

Dan and Sondra felt quite pleased with how well their moneytalk had gone. They had made some real progress: in communicating more evenly, in understanding each other better, and in taking some positive action.

CONCLUDING WITH THE COOL-DOWN

DAN: I appreciated how well you heard me, and that you were willing to set a concrete limit on your own spending. I know that's hard for you to do, and I want to tell you how much it means to me that you are willing to do it. I will also think more about working shorter hours to spend more time with you and the kids. I really would like that too.

SONDRA: I also appreciated your willingness to hear me so sensitively. Your openness made me feel safer with you and closer to you than I've felt in ages. And I was moved by your vulnerability in sharing your pain about money worry with me. I will try to be more conscious of my spending and talk with you about it more often.

SETTING A TIME FOR THE
NEXT MONEYTALK

Dan and Sondra agreed to sit down again one week after their vacation ended to see how the vacation went in terms of expenditure of money and communication about money. Both of them felt very good about their new way of talking about the thorny issues in their moneylife together.

Having

Your Own

Structured

Moneytalk

Here are the points to remember when conducting your own structured moneytalk on a loaded topic:

* Try to select a time for your moneytalk when you are not under a great deal of stress—not when the children are around, or when it's tax time, or when you have to make an imminent money decision. If you can't help but conduct a moneytalk when you are tired or stressed, remember that you will probably revert to old, somewhat dysfunctional behaviors because of this. Using structured communication will help limit the ill effects of stress, but it is not a magic formula. It is merely a set of helpful guidelines. The best way to prepare for a moneytalk is to be in a good and rested frame of mind.

* To choose an issue to discuss, turn back to chapter 7 and select one or two areas of polarization or chronic conflicts over money that you both would like to resolve. If you cannot agree on the same topic, each of you can choose one of your favorites, and you can draw lots to see whose topic gets discussed first. Using the suggested techniques,

you should be able to handle them both in the same structured conversation. Pay close attention to the feelings that surface as you decide on your topic. You will need to share them early on in the process of communicating.

* If you are holding on to any past hurts or angers, consider writing love letters to each other on the topic. If neither one of you has a pressing need to share the contents of your love letter, do not share this information but move on to the next stage of the moneytalk.

* If you tend to get frustrated communicating with your partner, and feel you are not heard often enough, practice "my perfect conversation" exercise as well. It will teach your partner what you need and want in conversations. You will also learn your partner's preferences in this regard.

* Agree on certain ground rules. I suggest adopting the ones that Dan and Sondra did, which I listed earlier in this chapter. Or return to chapter 8, and decide which ones would work best for your couple relationship.

The general order I would suggest for sharing is:

1. Warming up with positive strokes.
2. Sharing old grudges, hurts, and resentments.
3. Verifying your partner's feelings before going on to your own emotional reactions.
4. Negotiating for change.
5. Sharing positive cool-downs in which you validate your partner's efforts and your own as well.

If possible, decide on when you will meet for the next moneytalk. If you agree to take new actions, reward yourselves for your changes and monitor your reactions to them.

This highly structured process may seem laborious or artificial, and you might feel resistant to trying it, but I suggest experimenting with it anyway. You can always go back to your old communication habits at any time! I have found, in my twenty years of working with couples, that in most cases our usual ways of talking with each other about emotional subjects lead to win-lose discussions and misunderstandings, and can end in an explosion of blame and hurt feelings. Using these structured techniques creates safe boundaries within which to confront difficult feelings, and a process with which to resolve them.

11.

Goal Setting: Achieving

Mutuality and Money Harmony

Now you are ready for the final step in your journey toward money harmony: learning the skills involved in productive goal setting, first alone, and then with your partner.

If you are already feeling nervous and stirred up at the mere suggestion of mutual goal setting (telling yourself, "We want two different things; I'm sure we'll never be able to work it out!"), let me offer you some words of encouragement right off the bat. As experts in the field of conflict resolution have taught us, most people's goals, though they may be different from one another, are not actually in direct conflict.* If we take the time to communicate about our fundamental goals and needs, we will often be able to work out solutions that work well for each member of a couple. Goals that at first seem opposing may actually be only different from one another, and not mutually exclusive at all. So have faith

* Fisher and Ury's book is a primer for teaching win-win solutions.

that if you begin by doing your own good work to clarify your most important life goals, you will have the help you need in harmonizing your goals with your partner's later in this chapter.

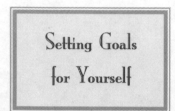

Before you attempt to discuss individual and shared goals with your mate, you need to learn about your own style of goal setting. You need to know whether you are able to envision and imagine goals you might have for the future; whether you tend to be a planner or a dreamer when it comes to addressing goals; whether you think about goals in terms of the near future, a few years down the road, or many years distant, or whether you are resistant to thinking about goals at all.

As for the goals themselves, you have to determine which of your goals persist over time, and which seem more fleeting; which goals involve you alone, and which involve your partner and/or your whole family; which goals involve money and would necessitate your coming up with more money; and finally, what steps—financial or otherwise—you would need to take to move toward the realization of your goals.

FANTASIZE ABOUT WHAT YOU WANT

How easy is it for you to envision or fantasize about what you want in your life? Some people love to do this. Others live in fantasy too much, and it prevents them from moving ahead in reality. Still others are afraid to imagine what they want. They believe in a kind of "superstition of pessimism": "If I let myself want something too much, I will be too devastated if I don't get it. It's better not to think about it at all." If this sentence describes you, you need to challenge this fear, and open up to the possibility of visualizing or imagining what you truly want in your life. Without being able to imagine it, I believe, you will be unable to achieve it. So when you are relaxed and at ease, take some time to let yourself conjure up pictures, feelings, sounds of what you would like to achieve or attain for yourself in the future. Do you want to take a trip to Paris with your partner? Would you like to buy a piano and begin taking lessons? Do you have a desire to go to graduate school? Do you want to train for a new profession? Or maybe just upgrade your computer? Whatever it is, give yourself permission to want it, first and foremost, with all your heart. That will pave the way for your being able to have it.

NOTICE YOUR NATURAL TENDENCIES AROUND GOAL SETTING

When you think about your goals, are they very short-term? For example, you may want to take a romantic vacation at a bed-and-breakfast with your mate in the next month or two . . . or buy something for your kids . . . or achieve something specific in your job.

Are your goals short-term (covering the next six months to a year)? Do you want to send your children to sleepaway camp? Do you want a new car? Do you want to begin putting aside more money for retirement or for the kids' college fund?

Are they mid- or long-term goals? Do you think about planning specifically for your retirement in five, ten, or fifteen years? Do you want to move in the next five to ten years? Do you think about changing professions or getting more professional training in three to five years?

Take some time to notice whether you tend to have goals that are short-term, mid-term, or long-term.

Now make a list of your goals, and for each one indicate:

- How soon you would like to achieve the goal.
- Whether it costs money to accomplish the goal.
- If the goal does cost money, how much more money you will need in order to realize it.
- Your ideas on how you might get the money to achieve the goal.

Try to think of a few goals that cover time intervals you tend to ignore. (If you're a short-term goal setter, for example, generate a couple of long-term goals.) Also, spend some time thinking about goals in areas you tend to overlook. (If you always focus on career goals, for example, come up with a few goals involving hobbies or vacations.) Notice whether you think about your goals in global, general terms, or plan them out in nitty-gritty detail. Whichever tendency you exhibit, try to do the opposite for a change, just to give yourself more flexibility.

If you have trouble doing any of this, I suggest you do the following exercise.

WRITE YOUR OWN IMAGINARY OBITUARY (OR AUTOBIOGRAPHY)

Write out (or tape-record, or think about and fantasize about in as much detail as possible) your own obituary, including all the things you want to achieve and/or have from now until the time of your death. If it makes you too anxious to go up to and including your death, do an autobiography instead, taking it into the future as far as you can. This assignment, which a creative client once brought to me, is astonishing in its power to clarify the kind of life you'd most want to have.

WHAT ARE YOUR SHORT-TERM, MID-TERM, AND LONG-TERM GOALS?

I recommend that you generate goals for yourself alone before considering goals for you and your partner together, and, if relevant, goals for the whole family unit. It's a good idea to divide these goals into three categories:

> short-term goals (up to one year from now)
> mid-term goals (from one to five years)
> long-term goals (over five years)

Again, specify when you want to achieve or attain these goals; whether it costs money to accomplish them; how much money; and how you might generate this amount of money.

Take the time to make this list of your goals, and the money involved in achieving them, *at least three times*. You can make the list once a week, every other week, or once a month. The important thing is to notice which goals come up time and time again. If you give yourself the time and space to generate a list of goals at least three times, you will have identified more trustworthy, abiding goals as opposed to impulsive fantasies that may change from week to week, or month to month.

ARE YOU SABOTAGING YOUR GOALS?

Do you tend to procrastinate? Do you feel fearful if things go too well? Are you afraid of having more pleasure in your life, or more educational status, or more wealth, than your parents had or have? If so, you might write out an imaginary conversation in which one or both of your parents give you permission to exceed them in some way. See if that helps reverse these patterns that may be holding you back from attaining some of your goals.*

I find in my therapy work and in my life that many of us are more afraid of new pleasure than of our old, familiar pain. Why? Because pleasure threatens to sweep us away into areas we haven't experienced before, whereas old pain is as familiar and comfortable as an old shoe. So we all need to work toward being able to "tolerate" new pleasure by letting go of our old pain, even though we identify with it so strongly.

ONE MORE LOOK AT YOUR GOALS BEFORE MEETING WITH YOUR PARTNER

A final exercise I would suggest is to look over the list that surfaced again and again, and to prioritize your goals in this way:

* Pat McCallum's remarkable book *Stepping Free from Limiting Patterns with Essence Repatterning*™ (Chevy Chase, Md.: Source Unlimited, 1992) maps out a process of mental reeducation that anyone can learn. It enables people to cast off the old "limiting patterns" that may be preventing them from achieving their goals, and to embrace new choices of attitude and action so that realization of life goals becomes possible, often for the first time. I have been using McCallum's process in my work with clients and have found it powerful and effective in creating shifts in consciousness as well as genuine changes—quite rapidly in some cases. (To order her book or her audiocassette contact Source Unlimited, P. O. Box 15826, Chevy Chase, Md, 20815.)

- Put a "1" after the goals that are the most important to you, the ones that you would be terribly disappointed not to meet.
- Put a "2" after the goals you want a lot but that you could live without if necessary.
- Put a "3" after the goals you could give up most easily, if you had to.

This is not to say that you can't achieve most or all of your goals. It is just a clarification of which ones are truly at the top of your list.

Make sure that for every goal you list, you have thought about the implications for your moneylife. Will it cost money? How much? And how will you go about earning, saving, finding that money in your budget? If you are a dreamer and not a planner, this part may be hard for you. But it is worthwhile to practice the nonhabitual by getting specific if you tend to be general and global. This will lead you closer to your goals.

After you both have done the work of fleshing out your own goals, both for you individually and for you and your partner together, you are ready to meet and share the results. You may want to sit back-to-back and share this information in the structured moneytalk format, announcing your intent to share, and asking whether your partner is willing to listen. Or you may feel comfortable enough to share face-to-face, without any structure. But if either of you panics upon hearing about goals you don't share, I would urge you immediately to go into the structured format, share your fears (if the other is willing to listen, of course), and try to mirror back what each of you wants, and how your partner is feeling about these goals.

Sharing Your Goals with Your Partner

It is crucial to remember that if you and your partner have different goals, and if you are both committed to trying to find a way for both of you to satisfy your deepest needs and yearnings, you will in almost all cases be able to succeed with this. Remember Mark and Kate, the planner-dreamer couple? When they first came to see me, he wanted to teach emotionally disturbed kids for almost no money; she was panicked, finishing her graduate degree, and worrying about how to put their daughter, Emily, through college if her husband pursued his dream. By slowing down the process, and tuning in to the planner's dreams (Kate's longing to live abroad) as well as encouraging Mark, the dreamer, to plan in detail how he would accomplish his dream of a career change, they happened on a dream and a plan they both could share: living abroad for a couple of years. During this time, Emily finished college, Kate finished her graduate degree, and Mark got some training in the field he was considering, to see if he would like it.

The final step is to merge your list of goals with your partner's. You'll end up with two sets of separate goals and one set of joint goals. The final goals should be such that both of you get most of what you truly desire. Remember to keep in mind how much money it would cost to realize these dreams, and to brainstorm creatively about how you might go about obtaining them. If you have doubts about being able to accomplish some of your goals, think about and discuss together alternative plans and dreams that might satisfy some of your yearnings.

Downsizing Your Goals in Times of Stress

One of the most difficult things to do, both alone and as a couple, is to have to downsize your goals, or put them off, because of financial hardships or other developments that you may not have expected or envisioned. Getting a serious injury or illness, being laid off at work, or not receiving any raises owing to the harsh financial climate can wreak havoc with your goals. In such cases, I recommend that you do the following:

- Sit back-to-back and use the structured communication format.
- Share your feelings of loss, pain, disappointment, and even panic about having to put off certain goals.
- Verify or mirror each other's feelings about this sad turn of events.
- Figure out ways for you to nourish yourselves during this period, both individually and together.
- Discuss how you *can* eventually achieve these goals; or modify them so as to make them more attainable.

Having a sense that your period of sacrifice is finite, and that you can substitute other sources of nourishment and pleasure for the ones that cost money you don't have, will help you overcome panic and move on to positive actions and attitudes.

It is my hope that after going through the process in this book, you and your mate feel safe enough with each other to do the following—and final—exercise. Spend a little time, each of you,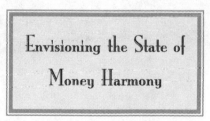

Envisioning the State of Money Harmony

fantasizing about and meditating on the state of money harmony. That is, consider how things would be if you felt totally at ease with your money, both in your individual life and in your life as a couple. If you are willing, close your eyes, breathe deeply, and come up with some mental images and sensations of this state of satisfaction and peace. What are some steps you could take right now to move toward this state? See if you are willing to each commit to taking at least one of these steps, either alone or together. If you do, reward yourself for taking this action, and monitor your reactions to it.

Congratulations for doing all the hard work involved in increasing your self-awareness and changing your behavior around money. Now you (and your partner if you have one) understand that money is not love, power, happiness, self-worth, or security—not even security in old age. Now you have the awareness and the techniques you need to communicate respectfully and creatively about your differences. You have learned to validate your partner's strengths as well as your own, to move toward the middle, and to practice "doing what doesn't come naturally" in your own relationship with money. Instead of having your money be an obstacle or source of tension, you can now use it as a tool to enhance intimacy and fulfillment in your life. I wish you well on your continuing journey toward money harmony.

Appendix A:

*Moneylife Quiz**

ead each of the following statements, and respond by answering "yes," "no," or "I don't know."

1. I have clear financial goals.
2. I have a budget or spending plan that is designed to help me reach my financial goals.
3. I feel comfortable with my spending habits.
4. I have a regular saving and/or investment plan.
5. I don't spend more than I earn.
6. I have an adequate system of financial record keeping.
7. I feel comfortable with the amount of savings I now have.
8. I know how much I owe to others.
9. I have at least one line of credit through a charge or credit card or other line of credit.

* The Moneylife Quiz was prepared by Helen and Bob Pelikan and Olivia Mellan.

10. My credit payments (excluding mortgage payments) are no more than 20 percent of my monthly net income.
11. I have an emergency fund equal to two or more months' net income.
12. I have life insurance or savings to cover my funeral expenses and all my other debts and financial obligations.
13. I have adequate health insurance.
14. I have adequate property insurance.
15. I have adequate automobile insurance.
16. I have a retirement plan.
17. I am willing to share the facts of my moneylife with close friends and intimates.
18. I am generally in harmony with my significant other in money matters.
19. I am financially generous with others.
20. I have a safe-deposit box for important financial records and documents.
21. I have a professional tax adviser.
22. I have a professional investment adviser.
23. I communicate with other family members about financial decisions.
24. I keep up-to-date on changes occurring in the financial marketplace that can affect how I manage my finances.
25. I am in control of my life around money; money doesn't control me.

This Moneylife Quiz is designed to help you find the areas of your moneylife in which you may need to do additional work. Take care not to use it to put yourself down in any way for things you may not have attended to thus far. Remember, self-flagellation leads to paralysis and inaction—not to progress. If you need the help of money professionals, refer to appendix B.

Appendix B:

Sources of Help and Support

FINANCIAL PLANNING

NAPFA is the national organization for fee-only planners. All NAPFA planners are required to be registered with the SEC and with the state in which they practice, to have at least three years' experience, and to have at least thirty hours of continuing professional education each year. In addition, they must have professional knowledge related to cash flow, insurance or risk education, retirement planning, estate planning, investments, and risk management. If you want a list of NAPFA members in your area, write to NAPFA, 1130 Lake Cook Road, Suite 150, Buffalo Grove, Illinois 60089; or call 800-366-2732. In addition, if you would like to order a sample interview form put out by NAPFA to help you ask the right questions when you search for a financial adviser, write to the organization and request the Financial Planner Interview Form.

If you are looking for a financial planner you can trust, I recommend you ask friends for referrals, contact NAPFA for fee-only planners in your area, and shop around, meeting more than one planner (three might be a good sample) until you find one whose credentials and experience meet with your approval, who has experience in areas tailored to your specific needs, and with whom you feel personally comfortable.

DEBT COUNSELING

Those of you who are struggling with overspending and/or debt may went to consider joining Debtors Anonymous. This twelve-step program operates free of charge and has more than 400 branches in forty-one states, as well as chapters in seven countries. Some local branches of Debtors Anonymous even specialize in couples issues. To contact the national headquarters, write to Debtors Anonymous, General Service Board, Inc., Box 400, Grand Central Station, New York, New York 10163-0400; or call 212-642-8220.

To find out if there are meetings in your area, call information and ask for Debtors Anonymous.

If you want practical advice on how to reduce your amount of credit card debt and arrive at a manageable payment plan, contact the Consumer Credit Counseling Service. By calling 800-388-CCCS, you'll get the address and phone number of the office nearest you.

Bibliography

THE PSYCHOLOGY AND PHILOSOPHY OF MONEY

"All Shopped Out and Nowhere to Spend? How to Know When Enough Is too Much." *Utne Reader,* September/October 1989, pp. 66–89.

Arenson, Gloria. *Born to Spend: How to Overcome Compulsive Spending.* Bradenton, Fla.: TAB Books, Human Services Institute, 1991.

Armstrong, Alexandra, and Donahue, Mory R. *On Your Own: A Widow's Passage to Emotional and Financial Well-being.* Chicago: Dearborn Financial Publishing, 1993.

Barber, Judy G. *Family Money: A Quarterly Commentary on the Unspoken Issues Related to Wealth.* Napa, Cal.: Judy Barber, M.A., Summer 1993.

Berg, Adriane G. *How to Stop Fighting About Money and Make Some.* New York: Newmarket Press, 1988.

Davidson, Bonnie. "When a Tightwad Marries a Spendthrift." *Working Mother,* November 1986, pp. 83–86.

Dominguez, Joe, and Robin, Vicky. *Your Money or Your Life: Transforming Your Relationship with Money and Achieving Financial Independence.* New York: Viking, 1992.

Felton-Collins, Victoria, with Brown, Suzanne Blair. *Couples and Money: Why Money Interferes with Love and What to Do About It.* New York: Bantam rack edition, 1992.

Felton-Collins, Victoria, and Wall, Ginita. *Smart Ways to Save Money During Divorce.* Berkeley, Calif.: Nolo Press, 1994.

Hallowell, Edward M., and Grace, William J., Jr. *What Are You Worth?* New York: Weidenfeld and Nicolson, 1989.

The Impact Project. *More Than Money: Exploring the Personal, Political and Spiritual Impact of Money in Our Lives.* Arlington, Mass.: The Impact Project. (Quarterly newsletter, available from 2244 Alder St., Eugene, Or. 97405.)

———. *Taking Charge of Our Money, Our Values and Our Lives: An Annotated Bibliography and Resource List.*

Katz, Donald. "Men, Women, and Money: The Last Taboo." Worth, June 1993, pp. 54–61.

Krueger, David W., ed. *The Last Taboo: Money as Symbol and Reality in Psychotherapy and Psychoanalysis.* New York: Bruner/Mazel, 1986.

Laut, Phil. *Money Is My Friend.* New York: Ivy Books, 1989.

Leon, Carol Boyd. "Going for Broke: Overspenders, Hoarders, and Achieving Money Harmony." *Washington Post,* June 12, 1990.

Lieberman, Annette, and Lindner, Vicky. *Un-balanced Accounts: How Women Can Overcome Their Fear of Money.* New York: Penguin, 1988.

Matthews, Arlene Modica. *Your Money, Your Self: Understanding and Improving Your Relationship to Cash and Credit.* New York: Fireside, 1993.

Mellan, Olivia. "The Last Taboo: Facing Our Tangled Relationship to Money," in "Money: Living with It, Living Without It." *The Family Therapy Networker,* March/April 1992, pp. 40–47.

Mogil, Christopher, and Slepian, Anne, with Woodrow, Peter. *We Gave Away a Fortune: Stories of People Who Have Devoted Themselves and*

Their Wealth to Peace, Justice, and a Healthy Environment. Philadelphia: New Society Publishers, 1992.

Mundis, Jerrold. *How to Get Out of Debt, Stay Out of Debt, and Live
Prosperously.* New York: Bantam, 1990.

Needleman, Jacob. *Money and the Meaning of Life.* New York: Double-
day, 1991.

Phillips, Carole. *Money Talk: The Last Taboo.* New York: Arbor House,
1984.

Phillips, Michael. *Simple Living Investments.* Berkeley, Calif.: Clear Glass
Publishing, 1987.

Phillips, Michael, and Rasberry, Sally. *The Seven Laws of Money.* New
York: Random House, 1974.

"Readers on WEALTH." *The Sun,* April 1989, pp. 123–28.

Romano, Lois. "Compromising Positions: The Tribulations of Post-30
Pairings." *Gannett Westchester Newspapers,* October 16, 1989.

Schmookler, Andrew Bard. *Fool's Gold: The Fate of Values in a World of
Goods.* San Francisco: HarperSanFrancisco, 1993.

Schneider, Susan Weidman. "Jewish Women's Philanthropy: What Do We
Need to Know?" *Lilith,* Winter 1993, pp. 6–39.

Seixas, Suzanne. "When a Spender Marries a Saver." *Money* magazine,
November 1989, pp. 114–24.

Sinetar, Marsha. *Do What You Love: The Money Will Follow—Discovering
Your Right Livelihood,* New York: Paulist Press, 1987.

Weinstein, Grace. *Children and Money: A Parents' Guide.* New York: New
American Library, 1975.

———. *Men, Women and Money: New Roles, New Rules.* New York: New
American Library, 1986.

"What Is Enough? Fulfilling Lifestyles for a Small Planet." *In Context: A
Quarterly of Humane Sustainable Culture,* Summer 1990.

"When a Hoarder Meets a Spender: How Couples Can Reduce Money
Stress by Diagnosing Their Differences." *Money Solutions.* Milwaukee,
Wisc.: Bank One Wisconsin Corporation, 1993.

Yablonsky, Lewis. *The Emotional Meaning of Money.* New York: Gardner
Press, 1991.

PERSONAL FINANCES

Altfest, Lewis and Karen. *Lew Altfest Answers Almost All Your Questions About Money.* New York: McGraw-Hill, 1992.

Armstrong, Alexandra, and Donahue, Mory R. *On Your Own: A Widow's Passage to Emotional and Financial Well-being.* Chicago: Dearborn Financial Publishing, 1993.

Cotton, Kathleen L. *Financial Planning for the Not Yet Wealthy.* Redmond, Wash.: FinPlan Publishing, 1987.

Feinberg, Andrew. *Downsize Your Debt: How to Take Control of Your Personal Finances.* New York: Penguin, 1993.

Godfrey, Neale S. *The Kids' Money Book.* New York: Checkerboard Press, 1991.

Hallman, G. Victor, and Rosenbloom, Jerry. *Personal Financial Planning,* 5th ed. Summit, Pa.: McGraw-Hill, 1992.

Jones-Lee, Anita. *Women and Money.* Hauppauge, N.Y.: Barron's Educational Series, 1991.

Lawrence, Judy. *The Budget Kit: The Common Cent$ Money Management Workbook.* Chicago: Dearborn Financial Publishing, 1993.

Lee, Barbara, and Siegel, Paula M. *Take Control of Your Money: A Life Guide to Financial Freedom.* New York: Ballantine, 1986.

Leonetti, Michael. *Retire Worry-Free.* Chicago: Dearborn Financial Publishing, 1989.

Lewin, Elizabeth, and Bernard Ryan, Jr. *Simple Ways to Help Your Kids Become Dollar-Smart.* New York: Walker and Company, 1994.

Loeb, Marshall. *Marshall Loeb's Money Guide.* Boston: Little, Brown, 1993.

Lynch, Peter. *Beating the Street.* New York: Simon and Schuster, 1993.
———. *One Up on Wall Street.* New York: Simon and Schuster, 1989.

Magee, David S. *Everything Your Heirs Need to Know: Your Assets, Family History, and Final Wishes.* Chicago: Dearborn Financial Publishing, 1991.

Martin, Mary E., and Martin, J. Michael. *Home Filing Made Easy!* Chicago: Dearborn Financial Publishing, 1993.

Miller, Theodore J. *Kiplinger's Invest Your Way to Wealth.* Washington, D.C.: Kiplinger, 1991.

Quinn, Jane Bryant. *Making the Most of Your Money.* New York: New York Institute of Finance, 1991.

Savage, Terry. *Terry Savage Talks Money: The Common-Sense Guide to Money Matters.* Chicago: Dearborn Financial Publishing, 1990.

Sinclair, Carol. *When Women Retire.* New York: Crown, 1992.

Wall, Ginita. *Our Money Our Selves.* Yonkers, N.Y.: Consumer Reports Books, 1992.

Weiss, Gerald, and Lowe, Janet. *Dividends Don't Lie.* Chicago: Dearborn Financial Publishing, 1988.

White, Shelby. *What Every Women Should Know About Her Husband's Money.* New York: Random House, 1992.

Woodhouse, Violet, and Felton-Collins, Victoria, with Blakeman, M. C. *Divorce and Money: Everything You Need to Know About Dividing Property.* Berkeley, Calif.: Nolo Press, 1992.

Wurman, Richard Saul; Siegel, Alan; and Morris, Kenneth M. *The Wall Street Journal Guide to Understanding Money and Markets.* N.Y.: Access Press, 1992.

COUPLE RELATIONSHIPS AND CONFLICT RESOLUTION

Farrell, Warren. *The Myth of Male Power.* New York: Simon and Schuster, 1993.

———. *Why Men Are the Way They Are: The Male-Female Dynamic.* New York: Berkley Books, 1988.

Fisher, Roger, and Ury, William. *Getting to Yes: Negotiating Agreement Without Giving In.* New York: Penguin, 1983.

Gilligan, Carol. *In a Different Voice.* Cambridge, Mass.: Harvard University Press, 1982.

Gray, John. *Men Are from Mars, Women Are from Venus.* New York: HarperCollins, 1992.

————. *What You Feel, You Can Heal.* Mill Valley, Calif.: Heart Publishing, 1984.

Hendrix, Harville. *Getting the Love You Want: A Guide for Couples.* New York: Harper & Row, 1990.

Keen, Sam. "The Blame Game." *The Utne Reader*, January/February 1993, pp. 65–68. Reprinted with permission from *Fire in the Belly: On Being a Man.* New York: Bantam, 1991.

"Men and Women: Can We Get Along? Should We Even Try?" *Utne Reader*, January/February 1993, pp. 53–76.

Mogil, Christopher, and Slepian, Anne. *Getting Along: Communication Skills to Help You and Your Loved Ones Move Gracefully Together Through Everyday Life.* Self-published through the Impact Project, 1992. To order, write to the Impact Project, 21 Linwood Street, Arlington, Massachusetts 02174; or call 617-648-0776.

Montagna, Donald. "Why Love Fails" (article & audiocassette). Washington, D.C.: Washington Ethical Society, 1982.

Rubin, Lillian. *Intimate Strangers: Men and Women Together.* New York: Harper and Row, 1983.

Tannen, Deborah. *You Just Don't Understand: Women and Men in Conversation.* New York: Ballantine, 1990.

PERSONALITY AND PERSONAL
GROWTH

Gordon, Thomas. *P.E.T. Parent Effectiveness Training.* New York: Penguin, 1975.

Hendricks, Gay. *The Learning to Love Yourself Workbook.* New York: Prentice Hall, 1990.

Jeffries, William. *True to Type.* Norfolk, Va.: Hampton Roads, 1991.

Keirsey, David, and Bates, Marilyn. *Please Understand Me: Character and Temperament Types.* Del Mar, Calif.: Prometheus Nemesis, 1984.

Kroeger, Otto, and Thuesen, Janet M. *Type Talk: The 16 Personality Types That Determine How We Live, Love, and Work.* New York: Dell, 1988.

Lerner, Harriet Goldhor. *The Dance of Anger: A Woman's Guide to Changing the Patterns of Intimate Relationships.* New York: Harper and Row, 1985.

———. *The Dance of Intimacy.* New York: Harper and Row, 1991.

———. *Women in Therapy.* New York: Harper and Row, 1988.

McCallum, Pat. *Stepping Free of Limiting Patterns with Essence Repatterning*™. Chevy Chase, Md.: Source Unlimited, 1992. To order, write to Source Unlimited, P.O. Box 15826, Chevy Chase, Maryland 20815.

Myers, Isabel Briggs, with Myers, Peter B. *Gifts Differing.* Palo Alto, Calif.: Consulting Psychologists Press, 1980.

Notarius, Clifford I., and Markman, Howard J. "Controlling the Fires of Marital Conflict: Constructive and Destructive Strategies to Manage Anger." A paper presented at the Maryland Psychological Association/Foundation Post-Doctoral Institute Workshop, December 7, 1990.

Index

Action
  negotiating change in, 173
Addiction(s)
  spending, 57–58, 78–79
Adulthood
  financial power in, 120–21
Allowances, 41–42
Amasser(s), 30, 32, 73, 87–89, 90, 95
  money dialogues, 100, 106–8
Anxiety, 50, 72, 85, 86, 103
  free-floating, 17, 38
Appreciation(s)
  mutual, 170
  of self and partner, 188–89
  sharing, 178
Assignments, 31–33, 48-49
  for amassers, 89
  for bingers, 82
  dealing with money personality, 74
  debunking money myths, 54–55
  for hoarders, 75, 76–77
  for money avoiders, 87
  for money monks, 84
  for risk avoiders, 94

for risk takers, 93
for spenders, 79–80
for worriers, 91–92
  writing own obituary, 212–13
Attitude change, 95–96
Attitudes toward money, 7, 18, 109,
  159
  differences in, 3–4
Autonomy, 149
Avoidance, 7
Avoider(s), 5, 30, 37, 73, 84–87,
  143–44
  assignments for, 32, 87
  money dialogues, 100, 103–4
  positive qualities of, 95
  see also Risk avoider(s)

Bargain hunters, compulsive, 81–82
Baseline, finding, 17–33
Becker, Rob, 113–14, 130–31
Behavior change, 95–96, 218
  negotiating, 173
Behaviors in relation to money, 7, 17–
  18, 109, 159

Binger(s), 73, 80–82
  see also Shopping binges; Spending
    binges
Blame(ing), 122, 134–35, 164
Boesky, Ivan, 61
Boundaries, 115–16, 152, 208
Budget, budgeting, 4, 74, 77, 85, 95,
  139

Childhood
  money memories from, 45–46, 179–80
  traumas about money in, 39
Climate of respect, 8, 136, 161–75
Cohen, Ben, 60
Communication, honest, open, 7, 157
  see also Structured communication
    format
Communication skills, 9
Communication style(s), 177–78
  male-female differences in, 120,
    133–36
Communication techniques (couples),
  161–75, 218
Compassion, 12, 136, 163
Competence, 119–20, 121
Competition
  among men, 114
  gender-based differences in, 116–17,
    128, 134
Confidence, defenses around, 121–22
Conflict, 4, 8, 12–13
  money, 191–208
Conflict resolution, 9
Consumer Credit Counseling Service,
  222
Control
  in family, 126–27
  money and/as, 4, 35, 61
Control of money, 117, 153–54
Cool-down, 174, 175, 205
Cooperation
  among women, 113, 114
  gender-based differences in, 116–17,
    128, 134
Corrupting influence of money, 44, 83–
    84, 105, 146
Couple relationships, 7, 10, 34–35
  financial power and, 121

male-female differences in, 113–14,
    115
  and money types, 74
  opposites in, 137–38
  power imbalances in, 127
Couples, moneylife of, 8, 9
Couples communication techniques, 8,
    161–75
Couples polarization patterns
  see Polarization patterns

Debt counseling, 222
Debtors Anonymous, 57–58, 78, 79, 80,
    222
Decision making, 126–27, 161
  see also Financial decision making
Decision-making styles, 127–28
Defenses, 198
  around confidence, self-confidence,
    and money, 121–22
  around feeling needy or vulnerable,
    117, 120
Delayed gratification, 78, 95, 139
Denial, 20
Depolarization, 138, 141, 142, 143,
    156–58
Depolarization process
  practicing steps of, 159–60
Deprivation, sense of, 46, 80, 108
Discretionary income, 124, 127
Divorce, 124, 132, 154
Dreamers, 141–43

Economic dependency of women, 124,
    125
Emotional backlash, 80
Emotional climate, safe, 162–64
  exercises for, 165–70
Emotional memories about money,
    45–46
Emotional needs, 4
Emotionally charged issues
  see Loaded issues
Empathy, 125, 147, 148, 158, 161, 163,
    174, 188
Exercises, 10
  debunking money myths, 53–54,
    63–64
  depolarization process, 159–60

Exercises, (cont'd)
   fostering positive emotional climate,
     165–70
   see also Assignments
Eye contact, 134, 173

Family(ies), 4, 34, 35–36
   financial circumstances of, 34, 38–41
   money memories about, 37–38
   money messages from, 106–7, 179,
     180
   power, control, and decision making
     in, 126–27
Family history
   and traditions around money and
     work, 42–44
Fantasizing
   about state of money harmony,
     217–18
   about what you want, 210–11
Farrell, Warren, 61, 124, 162n, 169
Fear(s), 17, 31, 38, 50, 72
   about money and work, 125
   sharing, 198–202
Feedback, 12, 165, 172, 203
"Feeling" type, 117–19, 129, 133, 134,
   195
Feelings
   sharing, 171–72, 173
   verifying partner's, 172, 174
Feelings about money, 17, 18, 31, 50
   talking about, 133
Financial advisers
   gender-based differences in selection
     of, 129–30
Financial climate, 5–6
Financial decision making
   gender-based differences in, 6, 116,
     117
Financial planners, 9–10, 85–86, 88,
   121–22
Financial planning
   sources of help, 221–22
Financial power in adulthood, 120–21
Financial status
   peers and, 45
Freedom
   money as, 50, 62–64, 72

Gamblers Anonymous, 153

Gay couples, 114, 126
Goal Setter A versus Goal Setter B
   polarization, 138, 155–56
Goal setting, 8, 209–18
   mutual, 115
   for yourself, 210–15
Goal-setting sessions, 128
Goals
   conflict/compromise, 155–56
   downsizing in times of stress, 216–17
   financial, 74, 77
   joint, 216
   long-term, 211-12, 213
   sabotaging, 214
   sharing with partner, 215–16
God, 108
Gray, John, 135, 162n, 168
Ground rules, agreeing on, 197–98, 207
Guilt, 17, 31, 72

Happiness
   money as, 50, 51–55, 72, 218
Healing styles, 116, 135–36
Hearing your partner
   practicing, 164
Helmsley, Leona, 61
Help and support, sources of, 221–22
Hendrix, Harville, 162n, 166–67
Higher Power, 108
History with money, 7, 33, 34–49,
   147–48
   of partner, 8
   structured moneytalks, 176–90
Hoarder(s), 4, 17, 19–20, 37, 73, 74–77,
   80, 90, 151
   assignments for, 32, 76–77
   description of, 30
   money dialogues, 100, 101–3
   positive qualities of, 95
Hoarder versus spender polarization,
   137–38, 139–41, 157–58
   structured moneytalk, 191–208

"I-messages," 162n, 164
Income disparity, 120–21, 123–24, 126,
   150–51
Independence, 4, 150
Intimacy, 8, 11, 132, 149, 190

Investment, 6, 18, 72–75, 78, 85, 88
    socially responsible, 83
    tips from friends, 129–30
Investment styles, 92–94, 128–29
Isolation, 70–71
Instant gratification, 4

Jeffries, Bill, 118
Job loss, 67, 90, 217
Joint/separate accounts, 131–32
    gender-based differences in prefer-
        ences for, 116
Jung, Carl, 117

Liquidity, 75, 78, 93
Listen(ing), 161, 174
    see also Willingness to listen
Loaded issues, 9
    discussing, 161, 170, 175, 187, 190
    structured moneytalk(s) on, 8, 206–8
Long-term goals, 211–12, 213
Love
    money as, 4, 50, 55–58, 72, 140, 192,
        218
Love Letter technique, 167–69, 192–94,
    207

Male-female differences, 8, 153–54
    around money, 113–26
    in avoidance, 85
    in burdens around work and money,
        123–25
    in communication styles, 133–36
    in decision-making styles, 127–28
    in fears about money and work, 125
    in investment styles, 128–29
    regarding merged/separate money,
        131–32, 149
    in selection of financial advisers,
        129–30
    in socialization patterns, 115–20
    in styles of philanthropic giving,
        130–31
Markman, Howard J., 148
Memories, 34–35, 45–46
    around allowances, 41–42
    about family members, 37–38
    about family's financial situation,
        39–40

Men
    burdens around money and work,
        123–25
    cooperation/competition, 116–17, 128
    and money as self-worth, 65
    and money management, 120
    moneyphobic, 85
    personal boundaries, 116
    power, control, decision making in
        family, 126-27
    selection of financial advisers, 129–30
    style of philanthropic giving, 130–31
    see also Income disparity
Message to partner
    announcing nature of, 164, 171
Mid-term goals, 211–12, 213
Mirroring, 174, 175, 187–88, 202, 203,
    215
Mirroring exercise, 166–67
Money
    burdens around, 123–25
    defenses around, 121–22
    family traditions around, 42–44
    fears about, 125
    meaning of, 4
    as root of evil, 44, 82, 105, 146
    talking about, 3–4
Money awareness work, 36, 37
Money conflicts, 191–208
Money dialogues, 8, 96, 97–109, 115
    how to create, 98–100
    internal commentary in, 98–99, 101,
        102–3, 104, 106, 107–8
    learning from own, 108–9
    sharing, 187
Money equals freedom myth, 50, 62–64,
    72
Money equals happiness myth, 50, 51–
    55, 72
Money equals love myth, 50, 55–58, 72
Money equals power myth, 50, 58–61,
    72
Money equals security myth, 50, 68–71,
    72, 75, 76
Money equals self-worth myth, 50, 65–
    68, 72
Money harmony, 5, 6–9, 13, 33, 109,
    158
    achieving, 209–18
    envisioning state of, 217–18

Money harmony work, 11, 13
Money history
    see History with money
Money management, avoiding, 7
Money Merger versus Money Separatist
    polarization, 138, 148–51
    see also Joint/separate accounts
Money monk(s), 30, 73, 82–84, 85
    assignments for, 32, 84
    money dialogues, 100, 105–6
    positive qualities of, 95
Money Monk versus Money Amasser po-
    larization, 138, 146–48
    structured moneytalk, 176–86,
    188–90
Money myths, 8
    assessing, 71–72
    identifying and debunking, 50–72
Money personality(ies), 8, 18
    assessing, 30–31
    dealing with,73–96
    dealing with problematic aspects of,
    95–96
    influences on, 34
Money Personality Quiz, 7, 20–29
Money personality types, 20, 29, 183–84
    descriptions of, 30
Money styles, 6
    acknowledging envies and apprecia-
    tions of partner's, 141, 157, 159
    of parents, 36–37
Money type(s), 7, 73–96
    positive qualities of, 95
Money Worrier versus Money Avoider
    polarization, 138, 143–45
    see also Worriers
Moneylife, 5–6, 18–19
    of couples, 8, 9
    influences on, 34
    moving toward harmony in, 31
Moneylife Quiz, 219–20
Moneylife vows, 45–46, 179
Moneytalks, 115, 125
    communication styles and, 133–34
    see also Structured moneytalks
Monitoring reactions, 11–12, 33, 49, 64,
    157, 159, 174, 207
Moving toward the middle, 142–43, 157,
    159

Mutuality, 209–18
"My Perfect Conversation" exercise,
    165–66, 207
    practicing, 194–96
Myers-Briggs Type Personality Indicator,
    117–18

Nader, Ralph, 60
NAPFA, 221–22
Needs and wants, basic, 63, 70, 72, 77,
    90
Needy feelings, 117
Negative patterns, 19, 49
Negotiation, 161, 171, 172, 173, 174,
    204–205
    in structured moneytalk, 204–5
No-interruption rule, 171, 174
Nonhabitual (the)
    practicing, 8, 145, 162–63, 218
Notarius, Clifford, 148

Obituary-writing exercise, 212–13
Obsession with money, 50, 88–89
Overspenders, overspending, 4, 5, 12,
    20, 37, 46, 82

Pacing oneself, 10–11
Parents, 108
    attitudes/behaviors toward money,
    35–36
    influence on moneylife, 108
    money messages from, 179
    money styles of, 36–37, 38, 101
Past (the), 33, 34–49
    preserving positive influences from,
    47–48
Patience, 12
Peers
    money messages from, 34, 45, 179
Philanthropic giving, 117, 130–31
Phillips, Michael, 70
Planner versus Dreamer polarization,
    138, 141–43
Polarization, 3, 206
Polarization patterns, 8, 136, 137–60
    gender-linked, 132
    summarizing, 158–59
Positive influences from past, 47–48
Positive qualities, 19, 163

Positive warm-ups
  see Warm-ups
Poverty consciousness, 146
Power
  in family, 126–27
  money as, 4, 35, 50, 58–61, 72, 87,
    146, 218
Power plays, 154–55
Power struggles, resolving, 137–60
Prioritizing, 4, 95, 138
  goals, 214–15

Relapses, 49
Relationship to money, 4–6, 7–8, 9, 97,
    109
  psychological aspects of, 6
  strengths and weaknesses of, 18–20
  troubled, 37
  values in, 36
Religious training
  money messages from, 34, 44, 105,
    179
Respect
  for differences, 136
  for strengths and weaknesses, 158
  see also Climate of respect
Response letter(s), 168, 194
Retirement, 75, 93
Reward(s), 12
  joint, 188
Rewarding new behaviors, 33, 48–49,
    64, 74, 157, 174, 207
Risk, 18
Risk avoider(s), 73, 92, 93–94, 95,
    128–29
Risk taker(s), 73, 92–93, 95
Risk Taker versus Risk Avoider polariza-
    tion, 138, 151–53
Risk taking
  gender-based differences in, 128–29,
    132

Saving, 4, 5, 72, 74, 139
Second marriage(s), 7, 186–87
Security, 75, 93
  money as, 4, 50, 68–71, 72, 75, 76,
    139, 140, 192, 218
Self-awareness, 18, 218
Self-awareness work, 7, 49

Self-confidence
  defenses around, 121–22
  training around, 119–20
Self-esteem, 12, 19, 57, 80
  increasing, 31, 49
  job loss and, 6–7, 67
Self-worth
  money as, 4, 35, 50, 65–68, 72, 87,
    146, 218
Setbacks, 49
Shame, 17, 18, 31, 72
Sharing
  feelings, 164, 165
  goals, 215–16
  hurts, resentments, fears, 198–202
  money dialogues, 187
  money history, 179–86
Shopping
  male-female differences in, 113–14
  as reward, 57
Shopping/spending binges, 36, 37,
    80–82
  see also Binger(s)
Short-term goals, 211–12, 213
Sitting back-to-back, 173, 174, 215
Social connectedness, 70
Socialization patterns
  male-female, 115–20
Society
  money messages from, 4, 34, 46–47,
    179
Spender(s), 4, 20, 73, 77–80, 139, 151
  assignments for, 32
  description of, 30
  money dialogues, 100–101
  positive qualities of, 95
Spending, 17, 72
  addictive, 57–58, 78, 79
  compulsive, 55–56
Spending plan, 77
Stress, 11, 206
  downsizing goals in times of, 216–17
Structured communication format,
    170–74
Structured moneytalks, 8, 128, 134,
    140, 206–8
  hoarder-spender, 198–206
  optional portions of, 186–88
  preparing for, 192–98

Structured moneytalks (*cont'd*)
  preserving safety in, 186
  sharing goals in, 215–16
  sharing money history in, 176–90
  tackling money conflicts in, 191–208
  using couples communication tech-
    niques in, 174–75

Taking credit, 134–35
Taylor, Elizabeth, 60
Teresa, Mother, 60
"Thinking" type, 117–19, 129, 133,
    134, 194–95
Topics to discuss
  agreeing on, 197
Twelve-step programs, 57–58, 78

Validation, 188–90, 218
Values, 34, 36, 61, 72, 83
Verification (feelings), 172, 174, 175,
    199–201, 202, 203
Victim versus Victimizer polarization,
    138, 153–55
Vulnerability
  defenses around, 117, 120
  gender differences in, 122

Wants
  fantasizing about, 210–11
  see also Needs and wants, basic

Warm-ups, 169–70, 173, 175, 177, 178,
    198
Warning of nature of communication,
    164, 171
Wealth, 146
  uses of, 60, 147
Willingness to listen, 164, 171–72
Win-win situations, 163
Women
  burdens around money and work,
    123–25
  cooperation/competition, 116–17, 128
  economic dependency of, 124, 125
  and money management, 119–20
  moneyphobic, 85, 121
  personal boundaries, 116
  power, control, decision making in
    family, 126–27
  selection of financial advisers, 129–30
  styles of philanthropic giving, 130–31
Women in workforce, 5–6, 65, 139
  making more than men, 7, 150–51
  see also Income disparity
Work
  burdens around, 123–25
  family traditions around, 42–44
  fears about, 125
Worriers, 4, 5, 37, 73, 89–92, 98
  positive qualities of, 95
Worry about money, 17, 36

Zimmerman, Isaiah, 162*n*, 170